THE
CHANGE PACT

THE
CHANGE PACT

Building Commitment
to Ongoing Change

PAUL STREBEL

FINANCIAL TIMES
Prentice Hall

PEARSON EDUCATION LIMITED

Head Office:
Edinburgh Gate
Harlow CM20 2JE
Tel: +44 (0)1279 623623
Fax: +44 (0)1279 431059

London Office:
128 Long Acre, London WC2E 9AN
Tel: +44 (0)171 447 2000
Fax: +44 (0)171 240 5771

First published in Great Britain in 1998

© Financial Times Professional Limited 1998

The right of Paul Strebel to be identified as
author of this work has been asserted by him in accordance
with the Copyright, Designs and Patents Act 1988.

ISBN 0 273 63294 9

British Library Cataloguing in Publication Data
A CIP catalogue record for this book can be obtained from
the British Library.

5 7 9 10 8 6 4

Typeset by Northern Phototypesetting Co. Ltd, Bolton
Printed and bound in Great Britain by
Biddles Ltd, Guildford and King's Lynn

*The Publishers' policy is to use paper manufactured
from sustainable forests.*

ABOUT THE AUTHOR

Paul Strebel is Professor of Change Management and director of the executive programme, Leading Corporate Renewal, to which executives bring live change issues, at IMD, the International Institute for Management Development in Lausanne, Switzerland.

He has directed a variety of in-company programmes for IMD's business partners and associates and has worked privately for numerous multinationals, including most recently, Schroders, Nokia, Nestlé, Bosch, World Bank and Coopers & Lybrand.

Professor Strebel is the author of *Breakpoints: How Managers Exploit Radical Business Change*. His publications have appeared in *Harvard Business Review*, *California Management Review*, *Strategic Management Journal*, *Handbook of Business Strategy*, plus many others, including numerous articles in the business press. He is on the editorial board of several change management journals.

Prior to his current position, he was director of research at Imede, one of the founding institutions of IMD. Professor Strebel is Swiss, of South African origin, received his BSc (Hons) from the University of Cape Town, his MBA from Columbia University in New York, and his PhD from Princeton University.

CONTENTS

Part II
ORCHESTRATING COMPACT RENEWAL

Part III
ONGOING COMPACT RENEWAL

ACKNOWLEDGEMENTS

The growing chasm between the demand for ongoing change imposed by a rapidly shifting environment and the ability of people on the front line to cope and commit, is at the origin of this book. Again and again, practising change leaders have focused discussion on this chasm. Since 1992, over three hundred managers have discussed their change action plans and related problems in the workshops that are an integral part of IMD's Change Program for executives. The files on these action plans, with follow-ups six months later in some cases and a small number of telephone interviews, together with my consulting experience, constitute the experiential raw material on which this book is based. Only a small number of these cases are cited explicitly in the book, several of them in disguised form to protect the identity of the managers and companies involved. However, the frameworks have been presented and discussed with most of the three hundred managers. I am indebted to them for the openness and spirit in which they participated in the Program.

The framework for relationships between people and the organization used in this book builds on the notion of a psychological contract, developed in the USA by Chris Argyris, Harry Levinson, and Edgar Schein. In addition, I have been influenced by several of my colleagues at IMD. The scheme in Part I for clustering people's response to existing change was inspired by an approach used in the classroom by my colleagues Jan Kubes and J B Kassarjian. The basic change processes in Part II echo the three types of change developed by Peter Killing. The importance of a learning compact in Part III grew in my mind on listening to Xavier Gilbert, while the notion of a leadership compact for change emerged out of numerous discussions with JB Kassarjian.

Apart from the case examples taken from the experience of the participants in The Change Program and my consulting, I have drawn on several cases published by current and ex-colleagues and students: Liisa Valikangas, Chris Lovelock, Sandra Vandermerwe and Brenda Sutton, JB Kassarjian, Morgan Gould, Nick Obolensky, Mike Stanford and Kate Blackmon, David Oliver, Don Marchand and Johan Roos. The reference details are provided in Appendix 2.

Editorially, I am indebted to Gordon Adler, the IMD Editor, not only for smoothing out the language in which this final draft is written, but especially, for helping me to make a transition from an academic style to being more direct. This was done on the prodding from Pradeep Jethi, Publisher at Financial Times Management, who insisted on a more user-friendly text.

Finally, I want to thank my wife, Biff, who drove me around during the months after I broke my knee skiing, the months during which the first draft was written, and then put up with several holidays being disrupted by revisions. Without her support this book could not have been written.

Paul Strebel
Lausanne, April 1998

NEW COMPACTS:
A COMMITMENT FRAMEWORK

The chasm is widening between the pace of change imposed by a rapidly shifting environment and the ability of people to cope. Chief executives are talking about total quality, lower costs, customer value, growth, innovation, and the multiple demands of the twenty-first century. And senior managers are making plans for process improvements in service, manufacturing, value chain management, and new flexible organizations for satisfying different markets and customers in the emerging, interconnected economy.

However, the people who are supposed to make it all happen, the people on the front line, are getting more and more confused and distrustful of management's intentions. According to a 1997 survey by the US-based Conference Board, mistrust of management and low morale were the biggest problems in employee relationships. A recent study in the UK reached the same conclusion: individual motivation and commitment in the mid-nineties were apparently lower than in the confrontational industrial climate of the mid-seventies.

The rapid pace of ongoing change disrupts commitment, because it is continually confusing the strategy, altering the task, and increasing the uncertainty. The problem is not merely the disappearance of job security. And the solution is not simply employability, although that is a piece of the puzzle. The problem is the increasing difficulty people have seeing how they fit in, reconciling a growing number of confusing change objectives with their job, acquiring an ever shifting range of skills. It is no surprise that front-line commitment is suffering badly in companies whose managers don't know how to deal with the individual fall-out from ongoing change.

To bridge the chasm and get people to commit to ongoing change, the change leader has to offer them new relationships with the company, relationships that translate corporate change to the level of the individual. What counts is not so much involving them in creating the change vision, but in linking the vision to what people do every day. Since real buy-in to change is an emotional, not just a rational, matter, individuals have to be able to connect the change to their own work situations, economically, socially and psychologically. To get people to support change because they believe it's in their best interests, not just the company's, you have to give them the chance to renew their relationships with the company on all dimensions, in the context of the new external environment. In so doing, you put them back in charge of their destinies.

These new relationships have to be total, in that they capture everything needed to support major change. I call these new total relationships new 'compacts.' The word 'compact' means 'an agreement supported by trust'. Although the word has other meanings, I use it to capture what is involved when employees and managers work with ('com') one another to create an agreement ('pact') based on trust.

This book, in three parts, will give you the tools for getting your people to agree to new compacts that support ongoing change. This involves building a bridge for people between the compacts they have today and those needed for ongoing change. The process of creating this bridge can be reduced to three steps (hence, the three parts of this book):

1. offer every individual an initial new compact that starts with where they are today, how they are responding to the current change effort

2. orchestrate the renewal of compacts with a process that builds on the company's change context

3. move from an initial top-down process to bottom-up renewal of

compacts – start renewing compacts from the top down, but once people understand what is involved move toward bottom-up.

WHAT'S IN A COMPACT?

A compact is a performance agreement (as reflected in a budget, action plan, performance review, etc.) plus a psychological contract and an employment contract. A performance agreement between individuals and their superiors typically covers the objectives and targets to be reached, and the resources needed to accomplish a specific mandate or task. The notion of a psychological contract, used by psychologists and analysts of organizational behaviour, refers mainly to the terms and conditions, the perceived rules of the game governing the relationship between the individual and the organization. The employment contract covers the legally binding aspects of the relationship.

Taken as a whole, a compact is shaped by the perceived obligations and commitments between the individual and the organization. Although employers and employees may not distinguish between the various facets of their relationship, nor necessarily spell them out, change leaders from a wide range of companies agree that a compact can be reduced to three main dimensions:

- economic
- social
- psychological.

The economic dimension

The economic dimension is the most visible one in the relationship between an individual and the company. It's the most explicit of the three dimensions. It specifies the agreement on the employee's tasks and performance targets, which are set out in performance agreements, action plans, business and budget plans, job descriptions, and employment contracts.

To get people to commit to a new economic relationship with the company, you have to address the key economic terms of their compacts. One of the most effective ways of doing this is to put yourself in their shoes and ask questions about how the change is going to affect their relationship with the company. Here are some of the most useful questions:

- *What specifically am I (the employee) supposed to do to support the change?*
- *What help will I get to do the job?*
- *What formal rules will govern the compacts, in particular?*
- *What feedback will I get and how will my performance be evaluated?*
- *What rewards will I get?*

When the individual's change objectives, for example, or the opportunity for personal development don't get special attention, their absence undermines the personal commitment to change.

The social dimension

The social dimension, in large part, shapes the emotional content of the relationship. It reflects the assumptions, values, and rules of behaviour the employee shares with others in the organization. Parts may be set out explicitly in statements of corporate mission, policy documents, and other written material. However, most of the social component has to do with management style and the organization's culture. Top-most in the employee's mind are questions like:

- *What vision will I share?*
- *What values will I share with others in the organization?*
- *What informal rules of behaviour and risk sharing will govern life in the organization? In particular, what kind of team or group will I be in?*

In many companies, unanswered questions on the social dimension cause commitment to wane. All too often, the rules that govern risk sharing are not articulated. Questions like who takes the salary cut when things go wrong are never clarified. Are conflicts resolved with formal rules and procedures, or politically? How are decisions made? Will you really be promoted for taking risks?

The psychological dimension

The psychological dimension is mainly implicit. It is the dimension where employees compare their perception of the benefits of the new compact in economic and emotional terms to their personal aspirations, needs, skills, and the risk of change. In short, the psychological dimension is where the employee judges the attractiveness of the compact. Questions that get at the psychological attractiveness of the compact include:

- *How good is it for me? Economically? Emotionally?*
- *How risky is it for me?*
- *What personal satisfaction will I get?*

Of course, the terms of the compact on the economic and social dimensions will shape your employees' answers to these questions. So, as a manager, you have to provide people with a new compact framework on the economic and social dimensions, that makes sense to them, that they can use to actually renew their compacts. Only this way will they be able to answer the questions on the psychological dimension positively.

In recent years, compacts have been becoming more explicit. A growing number of companies are addressing the relationship between the individual and the organization with explicit names, for example: At IBM, compacts have been called 'Personal Business Commitments'; at AT&T, 'Performance Excellence Partnerships'; at Philips, 'Personal Contracts'; at Goodyear, 'Individual Business and Development Plans'. There are several reasons for this trend. First, as companies become more truly multinational they become more culturally heterogeneous, and the risk of misunderstanding goes up. To reduce this risk, compacts need to be more and more explicit. Second, legal employment contracts are less and less a guarantee of job security, so employees, who are naturally becoming more concerned about how organizational change will affect their future employability, look for a more explicit form of compact to ensure that change is in their best interests.

The three parts of the book show you:

- how to design an initial compact framework that will appeal to people based on where they are today
- how to stimulate the actual process of compact renewal taking account of the company's change context
- how to move from top-down to bottom-up, employee-driven, renewal of compacts that supports ongoing change.

PART I: DESIGNING NEW COMPACTS

The first step in getting individuals to make a commitment to ongoing change is to offer them a new compact framework that is individually attractive, and reflects how they are behaving today relative to the current change effort. You cannot expect them to be attracted to a compact that is divorced from their current experience. Moreover, you have to appeal to them in a way that reflects their differing experiences.

But apart from the people on your immediate team, it is impossible to deal with everyone face to face. Yet, it is fatal to assume that everyone is in the same position – they're not. Employees can be grouped into at least four groups (or 'clusters') according to their reactions to a change initiative. If you want change to succeed, you have to address at least these four 'clusters' of players.

The change response clusters

- **Change Agents**
- **Bystanders**
- **Traditionalists**
- **Resistors**

In Part I of this book, we'll look (Chapter 1) at how to cluster people into these four groups. In the subsequent chapters (2 to 5), we'll take a look at what kinds of new compacts successful leaders offer these different players. In each case, the compacts have some features unique to the cluster in question. You'll learn that the key to designing attractive new compacts is to offer people tasks and rules of the game that build on the current behaviour of the cluster. Last, but not least, Chapter 6 shows you how to design your own compact with your boss and team.

PART II: ORCHESTRATING COMPACT RENEWAL

The second step in winning real commitment to ongoing change is to get people to respond to your offer by actually renewing their compacts. For this, you have to orchestrate/lead compact renewal so it brings the clusters of players on board successively, in a way that takes account of the company's change context. Obviously, the way you encourage people to renew their compacts in a crisis will be quite different from the way you do it during a period of growth. Four basic change processes exist for orchestrating compact renewal:

The four basic change processes

- **Top-down Turnaround**
- **Task Force Change**
- **Widespread Participation**
- **Bottom-up Initiatives**

Each of these four processes involves a different risk and, hence, each calls for different renewal tactics. Chapter 7 describes how to choose the right change process for a particular context. Chapters 8 to 11 then discuss the varying tactics of compact renewal for each of the four basic change processes, and Chapter 12 looks at how to deal with the politics.

PART III: ONGOING COMPACT RENEWAL

There is a third, critical step in getting people to commit to ongoing change. You have to build on their experience with the initial round of compact renewal. You essentially have to create the right conditions for a spontaneous, bottom-up process, which, in turn, allows people to decide on their own *when* and *how* they will renew their compacts. Giving your employees a greater sense of control over compact renewal, a sense that they are taking the initiative for change, is the final step in getting individual commitment to ongoing change.

The beginning of Part III (Chapter 13) shows you how to put together the change processes described in Part II to move toward bottom-up, employee-driven compact renewal. Then, Chapter 14 describes the social compact that best supports employee-driven change. Chapter 15 shows you how to transform employee-driven change into ongoing change by encouraging people to adopt learning compacts. Two are basic learning compacts:

The basic learning compacts

- **Efficiency Learning Compacts**
- **Innovation Learning Compacts**

In Chapter 16, you will see, however, that nurturing learning compacts is still not enough. To stay ahead of ongoing change and take the lead in today's rapidly shifting economy, top management has periodically to reorient the focus of learning compacts around the most relevant opportunities for value creation.

Taken as a whole, *New Compacts* breaks new ground. It highlights the role of compacts – the total relationship between an individual and a company – in getting the full commitment of people to ongoing change. It is also a guide to designing new compacts that provide significant perceived benefits to all major players. *New Compacts* helps you lessen the perceived risk of change by moving your organization towards learning compacts that support ongoing transformation. To lead your company successfully into the emerging, interconnected economy of the twenty-first century, you have to bring your people on board, but even more important, you have to let them lead the way. This book shows how.

Part I

DESIGNING NEW COMPACTS

The first step towards compacts for ongoing change is to offer people an initial compact framework that they can relate to, one that reflects where they are today. To do so, you have to start by taking account of their responses to the current change effort. Chapter 1 shows how to group people according to the two basic dimensions of an individual's response to a particular change. Chapters 2 to 5 then show you show how to design an initial compact framework for each of the corresponding basic response types. To complete the design of viable new compacts, you have to design a change leadership compact for yourself, as shown in Chapter 6.

THE
BASIC RESPONSES
TO CHANGE

GLOBAL ASSOCIATES: FROM LOOSE FEDERATION TO GLOBAL BUSINESS LINES

When Bob Jones became the new chairman of Global Associates, an international accounting firm, one of his main goals was to restructure the loose federation of regional firms into global business lines. His plan was simple: task forces at the top would work out exactly how the firm should be reorganized, how costs could be reduced, how new processes could strengthen Global's competitive position, and what key positions had to be filled. Then the recommendations of the task force would be rolled out. But when Jones started asking people to join the task forces, he got all sorts of reasons why the reorganization wasn't a good idea – especially from some members of the executive committee. Jones explained the advantages for the firm and the benefits for the individuals. The doubters wanted to preserve the status quo, and emphasized the risks. What Jones kept hearing was one underlying refrain: 'What's in it for us?'

Jones discovered, what many before him have discovered, that leaders cannot make people commit to change. Individuals themselves decide to commit – or not. Jones would have been better off if he had understood where his people were coming from, and offered them a viable new compact that supported his plans for change. With a more profound knowledge of compacts, Jones might have known what all change managers should know – among the large cast of characters who have to renew their compacts in response to a change initiative, there are some basic responses, that have to be addressed separately.

These basic responses can be thought of in terms of the energy in the employees' response to the change, whether they are active or passive, and the potential impact of the change on them, whether positive or negative.

5

- *The energy* is shaped by the uncertainty in the change and their attitude to risk. To provide a simple example, the risk takers are more likely to get actively involved, whereas the risk averse tend to be passive.
- *The impact* of the change depends on whether the change force in question is a personal threat or opportunity. The same individual will respond positively to changes that are in his or her interest and negatively to those that are not.

Although individuals are not locked into any one change response, everyone has a particular response to a particular change effort (active or passive, positive or negative). These responses cluster into types, each of which is associated with a behaviour pattern that provides managers with a reference point for designing new compacts.

This chapter will show you how you can group people into the basic types of change response, what tell-tale behaviour to look out for and, in the absence of a new compact, what people's likely response will be to a particular change effort.

CLUSTERING OF CHANGE RESPONSES

The players associated with change can be grouped using the two dimensions mentioned above:

- the energy in their response (active or passive)
- the potential impact of the change (positive or negative).

This grouping results in the four change response types shown in Figure 1.1: Change Agent, Bystander, Traditionalist, and Resistor. Each represents a typical combination of economic, social, and psychological factors that reflects the relationship between individuals and the organization.

Negative		
	TRADITIONALISTS	**RESISTORS**
	Security	Power
Potential	Loyalty	Position
Impact of	(Culture)	(Politics)
Change	**BYSTANDERS**	**CHANGE AGENTS**
	Recognition	Pride
	Participation	Accomplishment
Positive	(Mindset)	(Dynamics)

Passive	**Energy of Response**	Active

Figure 1.1 The change response types

To find the people in each group, you can ask yourself the following questions:

- To find the change agents ask: *Who is likely to respond actively to the force of change and see it as an opportunity?*

  These will be the change agents, with compacts typically driven by their own internal values and desire for accomplishment. They are activists, often already driving the dynamics of the organization, who see the potential for personal development in the change initiative.

- To find the resistors ask: *Who is likely to respond actively, but see the change as a threat?*

  These will be the resistors, with compacts typically driven by the desire to preserve their position and power. They are often senior managers skilled at playing politics to protect themselves. Alternatively, depending on the issue, they may be activists against a change initiative that threatens to disrupt what they are already doing.

- To find the bystanders ask: *Who is likely to be passive, even though the change is an opportunity for them?*

  These will be the bystanders, with compacts typically driven by the desire to understand fully what is going on and be recognized for it, before moving. They are often experts of various types who

7

need to understand the logic of the change, sceptics who have, or can easily acquire, the necessary skills, hampered by a fixed mindset, arguing about the merits of the change.

• To find the traditionalists ask: *Who is likely to be passive, and see the change as a threat?*

These will be the traditionalists, with compacts typically driven by a need for security and corresponding loyalty to the status quo. They are often middle managers, supervisors and others, who having learned how to work in, and to be comfortable with, the existing business structure, do not have the right skills to cope with the change.

When implementing change, you have to deal with all four responses. Yet, the mix, or proportion of each, can vary a lot from one situation to another: change agents and bystanders dominate in open organizations, whereas traditionalists and resistors dominate in closed organizations. Similarly, there tend to be more activists (change agents and resistors) when the direction of the change is clear and the uncertainty low, more passive types (bystanders and traditionalists) when the uncertainty is high.

GLOBAL ASSOCIATES: THE RESPONSE TO CHANGE

At Global Associates, the basic features of the existing compacts were typical of most change situations. It didn't take more than a few one-to-one discussions with selected partners for Jones to realize that several members of the executive committee were resistors. Each of them had been with the company for many years, heading a local firm of partners with the power to make their own policies, and with complete control over their region. If policies were to be harmonized across the regions, back-office logistics streamlined, and the organization restructured, these senior partners would have to give up power. They knew it and would probably fight hard to prevent it.

As a showdown between Jones and the executive committee loomed, most of the middle managers waited and watched – typical bystanders. Although many of them knew that if the chairman pre-vailed, they would benefit from new opportunities, they were passive for political reasons: they didn't want to risk taking sides.

An important minority of the partners and middle managers were in a traditionalist posture. A radical restructuring would disrupt their lives and, hence, would be negative for them. They kept their heads down, avoided the risk of involvement, presumably hoping that the whole reorganization idea would go away.

The only change agents Jones could find to join his task forces were younger partners, who sensed the potential benefits and were willing to take the risk of change. But he could barely find enough of them to make up the three task forces he set up to design the new worldwide audit, consulting, and tax businesses.

THE CHANGE AGENTS

In the typical fashion of change agents, the younger partners at Global Associates who were nominated to the task forces began meeting informally, well before the task forces were convened, to discuss how they would proceed. Some of the attractive features of the new compacts they had in mind can be summarized as follows:

A typical change agent compact at Global Associates was:

Economic dimension

What am I supposed to do?	Participate in task force to plan and manage change
What help will I get?	Support from chairman and task force colleagues
How will I be measured?	Based on performance, competence, commitment
What rewards will I get?	Possibility of new high potential career path

Psychological dimension

How good is it for me?	Very positive in terms of the opportunity to develop
How risky is it for me?	Not very risky, little to lose
What personal satisfaction will I get?	Challenge, ahead of the pack, creative, achieving

The chairman used the first meeting of the task forces to communicate his view of the change agent mandate and get buy-in to new compacts (you will see how to design new change agent compacts in Chapter 2). This was a smart move, since change agents see change as an opportunity to break away from the status quo. To take advantage of it, they like to move into action rapidly and get things done.

Change agents often respond to change by:

- stepping out ahead of the pack and away from the past
- moving into action as soon as possible to make things happen.

THE RESISTORS

Apart from the financial and organizational issues involved in reorganizing the firm, the burning issue for Jones was how to deal with the resistors on the executive committee, without creating such big waves in the organization that he lost the support of the bystanders and traditionalists.

The old guard executive committee members at Global Associates blamed Jones for stirring up trouble with all his talk about radical, global restructuring. They thought it unnecessary. The resistors did not buy Jones's views on the paramount importance of their global clients. In their estimation, it would have been enough to do some straightforward streamlining and cost reduction within the existing organizational structure. If the chairman succeeded, they argued, he would rip the organization apart. And that would have negative consequences for the people in the firm and society at large. Being a large player in a country, they said, carried responsibilities to a broader set of clients.

Determined to outmanoeuvre Jones, members of the executive committee lobbied their subordinates for support, making the point that reorganizing along business lines rather than geographic lines would destroy their local firms and expose them to new expertise requirements they couldn't meet. Since conflicts had previously been resolved by a show of political power with the blame falling on the loser, everything was done to put Jones in the loser's box. Even Jones's 'allies' on the executive committee held back to see which way the struggle would go.

The response of the resistors at Global Associates was typical. To get support, resistors go into competition with the change leadership. They try to convert traditionalists, bystanders, and even some change agents to their cause. If they succeed, the roles reverse and the change leadership finds itself in the position of resisting the resistors.

Resistors often block change:

- by looking for scapegoats
- by engaging in politics.

If you consider a typical resistor compact, it is easy to understand the reaction of Jones's opponents on the executive committee.

A typical resistor compact at Global Associates was:

Economic dimension

What am I supposed to do?	Run my local firm, co-ordinate resistance to change
What help will I get?	Persuade others to resist the change
How will I be measured?	Refuse firm-wide measures, local measures only
What rewards will I get?	Avoid being sidelined

Psychological dimension

How good is it for me?	Very negative, economically and emotionally
How risky is it for me?	Probable loss of money, power, and perks
What personal satisfaction will I get?	Nothing from the change, only alienation

Jones was convinced – there was no way he and the resistors could continue on the executive committee. He decided to force a show-down in the board room. After carefully preparing the ground, at the next board meeting he challenged the committee members one by one to declare their support for his global client strategy, or step down. Most supported him. That pulled the plug on the resistors, who had no choice but to resign. The way was clear for Jones to bring the bystanders on board.

THE BYSTANDERS

At Global Associates, ingrained assumptions about customer relationships and the competitive rules of the game created a barrier of bystander scepticism about the possibility of viable change. Having learnt the ropes during a long period of rapid market expansion, the local office managers were used to dictating terms to clients. It was difficult to accept client complaints about pricing, or that the competition really was providing more client value at lower cost. According to the bystanders, these problems were relatively minor, and would disappear once demand picked up.

Many of the local managing partners acted as classic bystanders, killing off most change proposals with a barrage of questions. Without realising it, they were undermining meaningful change and, thereby, blocking compact renewal throughout the firm. This was exacerbated by the earlier success of the firm, which made it difficult to accept that one could learn much from outsiders. External criticism was rejected as self serving publicity or competitive jealousy.

Bystanders often come from the ranks of those who provide the thinking for the organization; they want to understand and participate. If not, they withdraw to wait and see. The essence of the bystander resistance is the conviction that the change leaders have either got it wrong, or have yet to prove that they have a viable value creating idea. As a result, bystanders spend a lot of energy trying to persuade others that the change effort is misguided. They can be very creative about interpreting information to fit their existing compacts and their doubts about the viability of the proposed change.

Bystanders often undermine change by:

- refusing to accept the need for change
- questioning the logic of the change effort.

The typical bystander compact at Global Associates was:

Economic dimension

What am I supposed to do?	Protect integrity of our success formula
What help will I get?	Support of those who want to avoid dubious change
How will I be measured?	Performance, not in terms of dubious new processes
What rewards will I get?	Recognition for helping avoid illogical change

Psychological dimension

How good is it for me?	Benefits not clear
How risky is it for me?	Big risk it won't work
What personal satisfaction will I get?	Satisfaction of exposing a half-baked idea

Jones used the recommendations of the change agent task forces as the basis for the design and announcement of the new organization. The latter was communicated and its implications discussed at a senior partner conference, which was intended to bring the bystanders on board. The conference did not end until every managing partner present had an agreement with the chairman based on a personal action plan describing how he would implement the change. As the managers took charge of their new business units and responsibilities, they in turn had to deal with the large mass of traditionalists in the firm.

THE TRADITIONALISTS

At Global Associates, many of the front-line partners and employees sensed that the new organization, processes and skills would put them at a disadvantage, and they didn't like the uncertainty surrounding it all. Responding to the reengineering task force, they would say: 'My business depends on my personal relationships with my clients and the special attention I give them. Your approach may reduce costs, but it will depersonalize everything and I'll lose my clients'. To reinforce their position and to distract attention from the difficulty they would have fitting into the new global processes, they started offering their clients additional financial analysis as part of the audit package.

But the billing system, based on hours of time spent on a job, made it very difficult to charge clients for the value added by a service. Providing value-added services and getting clients to accept a corresponding change in the billing philosophy meant that the account managers would have to shift from their traditional role to that of a genuine consultant to the client. Being insecure about the latter, audit managers redoubled their efforts at getting as much out of the existing approach as possible. They tried to keep their clients on board by working longer hours out in the field. The audit managers argued not only that they didn't have the time to introduce the global processes, but also that the new systems wouldn't work in their market.

The large numbers of front-liners and employees who simply tried to get the most out of the old systems, rather than embracing the new ones, are typical. Why? Because traditionalists make up a large proportion of the response to many change initiatives. No matter what the change, most people would prefer not to be disturbed. Yet, they are a real obstacle to effective change, because their negative passivity saps the energy of the organization. From the traditionalists' perspective, the potential benefits of change are not there; the cost is too high. So is the uncertainty, which makes the idea of compact renewal completely unattractive. It makes more sense to them to capitalize on the benefits and security of the status quo.

Traditionalists often avoid change by:

- starting unrelated activities and projects
- redoubling the effort put into the status quo.

A typical traditionalist compact at Global Associates was:

Economic dimension

What am I supposed to do?	Satisfy my local clients with personalized service
What help will I get?	Continue to rely on a well trained regional team
How will I be measured?	Ability to maintain the regional business and clients
What rewards will I get?	New processes will erode compensated client time

Psychological dimension

How good is it for me?	My existing position is likely to disappear
How risky is it for me?	I may not fit into the new organization
What personal satisfaction will I get?	Insecurity dealing with uncertain change

15

As part of the new global organization at Global Associates, Jones and his team assigned many of the traditionalists to new tasks, with training where necessary. The changed assignments and training created a new security in the form of revised compacts which replaced the old way of doing things. With the traditionalists coming on board, Jones sensed that Global Associates had taken the first important step towards reflecting its name and fulfilling its potential. Observers inside and outside the firm attributed much of this first success to his willingness to listen to his partners and offer them appealing new relationships. To do what Jones did, you have to apply the key principles behind the design of new compacts for change agents, bystanders, traditionalists, and resistors. That's what you'll see how to do in the next chapters.

CHALLENGING CHANGE
AGENTS TO STRETCH

EISAI: THE POWER OF A CHALLENGE TO CHANGE AGENTS

How do you turn a pharmaceutical company into a health care company? Haruo Naito, the chief executive of Eisai, one of Japan's leading pharmaceutical companies, invited 103 middle managers to help him do just that. Naito gathered them at the Tokyo headquarters, where he introduced them to organizational change concepts and reviewed the trends in the health care industry. Then he sent them into the field, to help care for patients for three to four days in a geriatric hospital, and to visit a remote locality in Japan known for the quality of its local health care. Naito had a name for those who went: 'innovation managers.' They came back from the field profoundly moved by the plight of the aged and keen to lead health care project groups.

Almost without exception, the field experience transformed the managers into ardent change agents, proponents of geriatric health care products and services. In Mr Naito's words, 'They not only learned something new, they returned changed people'. The success of the geriatric health care projects (started by the first change agents), plus the recognition they got from Naito, immediately attracted others to follow. So much so that two years after the launch of the first projects, nine hundred people – a quarter of all Eisai employees – were involved in 73 old-age health care projects. Within a relatively short time, Eisai was moving quickly towards health care, tackling the twin threats of increasing competition in the Japanese pharmaceutical market and increasing uncertainty in pharmaceutical research.

What are the lessons for managers in Naito's approach? To design new compact frameworks that appeal to change agents, you have to challenge them to stretch beyond their normal routine, just as Naito did. Change agents are driven primarily by their own sense of self-worth, so the most powerful motivation for change agents is a chance to achieve and develop themselves. The support created for innovation projects at Eisai illustrates just how much this challenge can produce. No matter how charismatic or effective change leaders may be, they have to offer change agents new compacts that will rally them to their side. This chapter will help you offer your change agents attractive new compacts, by showing you how to:

- get their attention
- design an attractive new compact framework for them
- anticipate when they will need help in their personal process of commitment.

GET YOUR CHANGE AGENTS' ATTENTION

However you choose to draw the attention of the change agents to the change effort, it has to open up a dialogue. To start that dialogue, you have to take account of the degree of openness in the organization. You must remember that the early phases of the compact design process are crucial, because if change agents don't like what they see and hear, they can very easily land in the camp of the reisistors. In the early phases, first contacts and impressions often determine whether or not they are willing to renew their compacts.

The discreet approach to change agents in a closed company

It is difficult to find change agents in organizations that are closed to change. Not surprisingly, traditionalists and resistors walk their corridors, blocking change at every turn. To avoid alienating everybody with talk of change, you have to use a subtle approach. You can, for example:

- recruit change agents discreetly
- use a defining event to signal that they can come forward.

Public solicitation in a partially open organization

In organizations where at least a few change agents are already operating in the open, you can solicit the support of change agents publicly. Numerous approaches are possible. You can:

- approach the change agents directly
- ask managers to nominate change agents to task forces.

At Eisai, some change agents were already operating openly, so Naito solicited the support of more change agents publicly, simply by inviting his 103 managers to join the geriatric field program. At the first meetings, he unabashedly asked the members of his audience to help implement change by mobilizing and leading project groups. This public approach was only possible because he already had a task force of committed people looking at Eisai's future. *They* had come up with the option of geriatric care, so by the time Naito called for support, others in the company at large had already heard the idea and were aware that change was in the air.

Nurturing of many change agents in an open organization

Companies that are open to change manage to sustain many change agents over time by offering them compacts that evolve continually. Such companies involve change agents in ongoing change: they give them freedom, resources and contacts. When the company needs a change effort, the change agents are already at full attention.

DESIGNING A NEW COMPACT FRAMEWORK FOR CHANGE AGENTS

Without a new personal compact to back it up, the invitation to be a change agent is meaningless. Change agents need to revise the answers to the questions that make up their compacts in a way that challenges them and, to be productive, the compacts have to support the overall change objectives. For that to happen, you need to design two kinds of change agent compacts – those for your *task-oriented* change agents, and those for your *people-oriented* change agents.

- *Task-oriented change agents* – task-oriented change agents tend to be good at fleshing out the formal economic dimension of new compacts with others, but poor at interpersonal relations. At Eisai, many of the first people who set up geriatric health care projects were so focused on project technicalities that they had difficulty maintaining the outwardly harmonious relations which normally characterize Japanese team work.
- *People-oriented change agents* – people-oriented change agents, who are just as important as task-driven agents, are skilled at aligning the compacts of others with the stated change objectives of the firm. At Eisai, the project leaders with problems got help from team members and others who were more adept at interpersonal relations. Both types of change agent, however, were crucial to the success of the team efforts.

Compact features that typically appeal to the two change agent types are listed together in Figure 2.1.

	Task-oriented change agents	People-oriented change agents
Economic dimension Challenge to stretch based on:	A task worth doing	Acting as a facilitator
Social dimension Organizational space to:	Experiment and achieve	Coach and develop teams
Psychological dimension Enhance self-worth with:	Opportunity to accomplish	Opportunity for self-development

Figure 2.1 Compact features that appeal to change agents

For both the task-oriented and people-oriented change agents, the managerial challenges in the design of change agent compacts are summarized in Figure 2.2.

	Task-oriented change agents	People-oriented change agents
Economic dimension	Manage the risk implicit in their freedom	Get them to be more economically oriented
Social dimension	Create separate rules of the game for them	Help them manage conflicts with appropriate guidelines

Figure 2.2 Managerial challenges in the design of change agent compacts

In compacts for task-oriented change agents, you have to manage the risk in the freedom you give them. In compacts for people-oriented change agents, you have to provide guidelines to help them reduce the risk in personal conflicts their intervention may well cause.

THE COMPACTS FOR CHANGE AGENTS AT EISAI

Haruo Naito wanted his task-oriented change agents to be willing to develop new business opportunities. But developing new business is a high risk activity with a low rate of success. To get change agents to accept the challenge, Naito had to nurture a social compact that included acceptance of failure in the informal rules of the game. After change agents had taken the seminar on the health care trends and completed the field work on geriatric care, Naito gave them a challenge: propose a project that will help turn our new health care vision into reality. He gave them freedom to determine most of the terms in their new compacts, to set up and run the projects as they saw fit, without any threat to their job security if they failed. In effect, Naito offered them new compacts that were based mainly on the challenge in the task. The key elements of these compacts can be summarized as follows:

Economic dimension

What am I going to do?	Develop a health care idea with a team
What help will I get?	Whatever resources I need
How will I be measured?	Report to Mr Naito twice a year
What rewards will I get?	Chance to run a business

Social dimension

What vision will I share?	Dedication to health care
What values will I share?	New set of entrepreneurial values
What informal rules will apply?	A lot of freedom within Eisai business standards

Psychological dimension

How good is it for me?	A new career opportunity backed by the CEO
How risky is it for me?	Even if I fail, I'll get credit for trying
What personal satisfaction will I get?	Lead team and turn product idea into reality

The psychological attraction of this compact is clearly in the opportunity to start up something new with a lot more freedom than is usual in a Japanese business setting. Projects ranged from new marketing concepts (such as helping hospitals to improve patient care, and shifting the promotion of drugs from their medical properties to their impact on the quality of the patient's life) to the pursuit of opportunities in geriatric care (such as the development of drugs for the elderly).

HELPING CHANGE AGENTS TO COMMIT

Even though change agents like taking the initiative, they will not automatically buy into new compacts. Change efforts can be permanently grounded before they take off – by misunderstanding, or lack of full commitment on the part of the very people the change manager is relying on to spearhead the effort. There are several points in the individual process of compact revision where you should be ready to help change agents commit:

- *When they become aware of a new change initiative, change agents may go through a dip in morale.* This happens when they believe that their existing projects will be negatively affected. Change agents usually try to restore morale by downplaying the importance of the new initiative. This is a critical point. When you hit it, you have to challenge the change agents to get involved in the new initiative by putting existing efforts in perspective and, if necessary, lowering their priority.

- *Once the change agents understand what the change priorities are, they have to decide whether to participate.* During this period of indecision, you have to communicate the challenge and excitement in the change initiative. If you can get your enthusiasm across, so that your change agents can see and feel the potential benefits of the project, they will be keen to renew their compacts.

- *To ensure that the change agents buy in, you have to give them the opportunity to signal their commitment.* You have to provide each change agent with the opportunity to accept the new compact. In general, buy-in occurs when a change agent agrees to lead a task force, run an experiment, or do whatever is needed to get the change started. Successful buy-in is mutual. In return for the change agent's commitment, you have to promise to deliver the necessary resources and support.

COMMITMENT AT EISAI

At Eisai, the buy-in occurred at the end of the health care seminar. Each of the managers who attended the health care innovation program had to make a presentation to the company board at the end, describing how he had been affected, and what the implications were for the Eisai vision. In effect, each had to explain how his project would help turn the new Eisai vision into reality. This was tantamount to expressing his commitment to the new vision publicly. The manager's project proposal inevitably put his reputation on the line. And Naito's acceptance committed the company to providing the necessary resources and organizational flexibility.

To unleash the full power of change agents, you have to give them the maximum freedom possible, without jeopardizing the cohesion of the change effort. With the freedom to design most of their own compact, change agents will take greater ownership and responsibility for the outcome of the change effort. This feeling of responsibility for the outcome means that there is less need for detailed follow-up.

At Eisai, with the large bottom-up role played by change agents in the design of their compacts, there was little need for formal follow-up. Once the first innovation projects were up and running, there was full identification with, and commitment to, the objectives of the change effort from the change agents. They generated a network of self-organizing teams dedicated to health care. Apart from the twice yearly progress reports that he got on the projects, Naito saw his follow-up role as being the facilitator of 'corporate knowledge creation' at the centre of the network of teams. In this role, he could both monitor and guide the work of the teams.

The ultimate reason for monitoring the performance of change agents is to further the progress of the total change effort. The objective of change agent activity is to get the task-oriented change agents to help define the value-creating idea and its implications, while the people-oriented change agents help to initiate compact renewal in the rest of the organization. Whatever the momentum created by change agents, however, at some point the change leadership has to bring the bystanders on board.

MOBILIZING
BYSTANDERS
WITH THE
VALUE-CREATING LOGIC

FEDERAL EXPRESS: CLEAR GOALS TO BRING BYSTANDERS ON BOARD

'We concluded that what we needed for Federal Express were three very simple goals', with incentives, to move the divisional managers. Tom Oliver, Senior Vice-president Sales and Customer Service at Federal Express, had been facing a wall of bystander indifference when he tried to deal with service bottlenecks. Although the divisional managers would have benefited from improved service quality, they were not convinced. Most chose to behave as bystanders on the matter of cross-divisional quality improvement, preferring instead to maximize the performance of their own divisions. This 'resulted in a deterioration of the performance for the (FedEx) system. We realized that the more each unit tried to maximize its own performance, the more it tended to send difficult problems downstream.' Consultants were brought in to spearhead a service improvement program. They designed and led quality planning workshops for all the senior executives, helped set priorities and produce action plans. Task-oriented change agents were identified to head the quality action teams, and a network of facilitation change agents, 'quality professionals', was established throughout the company. Yet, progress was fragmented.

To remove bystander scepticism and bring them on board, you have to offer them a crystal clear compact framework. You have to demonstrate how the value-creating logic will affect them personally (the value-creating idea must be obvious, and supported by incentives and resources, so it can be seen as feasible). Bystanders want to know how they will fit in and be recognized and rewarded for their contribution.

DESIGNING A NEW COMPACT FRAMEWORK FOR BYSTANDERS

The compact features that appeal to bystanders are shown in Figure 3.1:

Economic dimension	A strong value-creating idea with a clear understanding of how one will fit in and be rewarded, and the resources available for implementation
Social dimension	A clearly communicated change vision, with accompanying values and rules of the game
Psychological dimension	Ability to identify with the change vision and see the potential personal benefits in the change

Figure 3.1 Compact features that appeal to bystanders

To design these features into new compacts, you have to build them into answers to the compact questions.

A crystal clear value-creating idea

(What am I supposed to do?)

When bystanders ask, 'What can I do to support the change effort?' the answer must be straightforward and easy to get. This means crystallizing the change vision in a value-creating idea, possibly a slogan, or simple goals, but in any case, a focal point to which bystanders can relate their new compacts.

Over the years, Federal Express had used a series of clear goals to focus various change efforts. They started with the slogan: 'Federal Express. Twice as Good as the Best in the Business'. This provided a benchmark for comparing Federal's performance against the leading competitor at the time, Emery Air Freight, and served as the basis for an external image-building campaign. As Federal drew away from

Emery, it captured its drive for reliability in the now classic slogan 'Absolutely, Positively Overnight' and the simple equation 'Q=P' (quality equals productivity), which linked productivity with doing things right the first time .

To focus the improvement effort in service quality, Federal concentrated on three dimensions:

- service quality
- people leadership
- profits.

The company developed a special Service Quality Index (SQI, pronounced 'sky') based on the findings of extensive customer research. A new slogan was developed, urging employees to 'Reach for the SQI'!

Key performance indicators linked to the value-creating idea
(How will I be measured?)

Bystanders want to know how they will fit in. To satisfy this need, you have to provide key performance indicators that are not only derived from the value-creating idea, but that also relate directly to the contribution the bystanders are expected to make.

To this end, Federal Express targeted a 20 per cent improvement on their SQI Quality Index (basically a 'hierarchy of errors' based on 12 different events that occurred many times every day and could go wrong). In addition, they used the already existing leadership index, SFA (Survey Feedback Action based on a confidential survey of a manager's employees), as the single goal for each manager in the people management process, but for the first year of the quality improvement program, Federal increased the SFA target only slightly. For the profit goal, management set a target of 10 per cent operating margin for the domestic business. With these three targets in place, everyone at Federal knew where to put their effort – solidly behind the collective effort.

Convincing commitment of resources
(What help will I get?)

Bystanders should not have to ask what help they will get. The amount of resource committed to make the change happen – in people, training, and money – should make the answer obvious. A company's commitment should be so evident that sceptics have little room to question the feasibility of the effort. So the test is whether the change is deemed do-able by bystanders on the front line.

At Federal Express, top management did not ask people to reach for the quality improvement targets in a vacuum. Consultants led senior executives from all the divisions through planning workshops, trained the managers in the sale and service division, and the employees and facilitators from other divisions, including ground operations. The training programmes incorporated five modules covering all aspects of quality management for the managers, and quality improvement for the employees. In addition, the consultants set up 12 quality action teams and trained them in implementing quality, with a focus on the components of the SQI Index. Nobody could say that there wasn't enough help to support quality improvement.

Economic rewards tied to the achievement of the key performance indicators
(What rewards will I get?)

Bystanders want the sense that they will be rewarded economically, if not now, then in the future, for their contribution to the change effort.

Federal Express (FedEx) linked part of the compensation package to the achievement of the change targets. Senior management announced that there would be no bonus for any manager, unless the company achieved all three of its corporate targets. According to Tom Oliver, 'It was very different from our previous approach of having managers' bonuses based on their ability to meet individual management by objective goals without regard to whether that did or didn't help the corporate process. In the actual unfolding of the change, last year turned out to be the best year we had had in a long time on all three measures'. The quality index target went beyond target by 15 per cent. The leadership index recorded the largest single jump in the history of measuring managers' relationships with employees. And FedEx achieved its profit goal, despite difficult circumstances. 'Needless to say', according to Tom Oliver, 'linking the bonuses to the corporate change objectives caught everyone's imagination'.

Values consistent with the change vision
(What values will I share?)

The redesign of bystander compacts will fail if it is not consistent with the values reflected in the organization. The latter provide hidden, and therefore powerful, signals about what management really believes is important, as opposed to what that management says is important. Managerial credibility is at stake.

For some time, Federal Express had been nurturing the values needed to support a service quality initiative with several awards. Fred Smith, the CEO, had initiated the 'Bravo Zulu' awards (meaning Well Done!) which provided managers with a way of giving instant recognition for excellent service within the company. 'Golden falcon' awards, consisting of a gold pin and ten shares of Federal Express stock, recognized outstanding customer service. To motivate others to join in, the company publicized the awards. In addition, to reinforce the quality improvement effort, management initiated quarterly awards for best performance in four categories:

1. Greatest impact on SQI results.
2. Best use of the quality process (using the tools that had been taught).
3. Best understanding of root causes (identifying and working on underlying problems rather than superficial effects).

4. Best use of employee input (gathering information from the people closest to the process who knew it best).

Participation that reinforces the change objectives
(What informal rules will apply and what kind of team will I be in?)

Meaningful participation is important for everyone, but especially important for bystanders. Before bystanders will throw their full weight behind the effort, however, they need some confidence that their contribution will not get lost in the shuffle. By divulging the rules governing participation in the change effort and the kind of teams that people will be in, you can cement the commitment of your bystanders.

At Federal Express, those who joined the quality action teams got the active support and encouragement of the chief executive himself. Moreover, a vice-president headed most of the action teams. Reports of the teams' activities and accomplishments went onto bulletin boards every week. And every three months, the teams reported to the chief executive and his team, directly. On the other hand, the parts of the service quality programme without clear rules of engagement attracted less support. 'We really have to push the notion of (internal) customer-supplier alignment. People and departments don't always work well together.' Yet, once management put a reward system in place to encourage people to report the details of their successes, thereby signalling the importance of internal customer-supplier relationships, more bystanders joined in. The situation improved markedly – many more people volunteered for initiatives to improve internal customer-supplier alignment.

THE NEW BYSTANDER COMPACT AT FEDERAL EXPRESS

When the message on all of the compact questions fits together, it provides a powerful framework for an attractive new bystander compact.

It is easy to see the appeal of the new compact framework for the divisional managers at Federal Express from the following summary:

Economic dimension

What am I supposed to do?	Focus on the corporate targets, especially the SQI index
What help will I get?	All the expert advice needed, plus the support of my peers
How will I be measured?	Contribution to achieving the three corporate targets
What rewards will I get?	A bonus tied to the achievement of the three targets

Social dimension

What vision will I share?	Significant cross-divisional improvement in customer service
What values will I share?	Importance of people, service, and profits
What informal rules will apply?	Strong recognition of quality improvement performance

Psychological dimension

How good is it for me?	Easier to achieve my unit and personal objectives
How risky is it for me?	Little personal risk because this is a collective effort
What personal satisfaction will I get?	Contributing to a real difference in FedEx's performance

An important point in this compact is the way management used key performance indicators to focus the change vision and link it tightly to individual compacts. This kind of clarity reduces the uncertainty in the change process, and thereby appeals to the logic of bystanders who typically are sensitive to the trade-off between the risk and potential return associated with change.

HELPING BYSTANDERS TO COMMIT

Unfortunately, all too often, change managers neglect to ask bystanders to commit explicitly, assuming that once they have communicated clearly, the rest will happen on its own: people will pick up the cause of change and drive the process forward. This ignores the different psychological triggers that motivate people (change agents, traditionalists and resistors are unlikely to respond to value-creating logic alone). And even with respect to bystanders who do respond to a clear value-creating idea, firms have to be sensitive to the individual process of compact design and the importance of giving them a chance to signal their commitment.

As in the case of change agents, bystanders may need help with several points in the individual process of compact renewal:

- *The first description of the value-creating idea is critical.* Like everyone else, bystanders may experience a drop in morale when they become aware of your agenda. Their first impulse is to generate all sorts of reasons and explanations for why the change is not really necessary and will be counterproductive. To reduce this first negative impact, you cannot afford to talk about change lightly. What might tickle the interest of change agents can trigger a lot of defensive resistance elsewhere. Clear communication of the value-creating idea is essential.

- *The framework for a complete new compact must be put on the table.* Once bystanders understand the change priorities, they typically examine the value-creating idea to see whether it hangs together and whether they can fit into the project. When they see that the value-creating idea cannot be derailed by argument, they often negotiate to see whether the project can be adapted to their views. If this tack fails, they may become alienated from the change leadership, before they finally accept that they have to accommodate the change effort. This phase of negotiation and possible alienation can be shortened if the framework you provide for a new compact is complete, as outlined in the previous section, thereby pre-empting many of the questions bystanders normally raise.

- *You will have to find out whether the bystanders are willing to commit*, whether they want to play a change agent role, or whether they prefer a more typical bystander compact, in a supporting role. You can provide bystanders with the same kinds of signalling opportunities you offer change agents: concrete opportunities for them to get involved in the change process, for example, by leading, or participating in a change project, or acting as a change co-ordinator, or sponsor.

At Federal Express, individual bystanders signalled their commitment by sponsoring or joining the quality improvement teams. In each training workshop, senior executives produced a series of written action plans, setting priorities on the problems that needed resolution. No matter what the change, in general, there is no substitute for a clear signal of commitment. To bring as many bystanders as possible on board, you will have to make it crystal clear in concrete terms what the change aims to accomplish and how the bystanders can participate. And then you will have to provide the opportunity for them to signal their buy-in. Explicitly.

INVOLVING TRADITIONALISTS IN A NEW REALITY

SUN LIFE: TURNING A TRADITIONALIST SALES STAFF INTO CASE MANAGERS

John Reeve, CEO of Sun Life, the UK pension, life and investment company, wanted to be Number One in the UK broker market. To get there, his re-engineering team proposed an integrated approach to customer service that would be provided by case managers with 'end-to-end' responsibility for customer accounts. The case manager would handle/co-ordinate all aspects of a customer relationship and all the transactions for a particular product. These case managers would work in 'cross-skilled' teams, whose members would back each other up in their transactions on different products. To test out the new design, Sun Life launched a pilot project run by change agents from three of the company's 40 branch offices.

The pilot projects ran into strong passive resistance from the sales staff who had been serving the brokers out of the branch offices. The sales staff had been spending about 40 per cent of their time sorting out problems with the brokers and relaying questions about the products back and forth between headquarters and brokers. With the integrated approach, many sales people would have to change their behaviour and acquire new skills to become case managers; if they didn't, the change would be negative: they would lose their jobs. The transition would require a big shift in attitude, skills and behaviour, so they responded as classic traditionalists: they did their best to avoid having anything to do with the pilot projects.

To bring traditionalists on board, you have to offer them new compacts based on the alternative security of a new, functioning work environment, with the necessary skills training to get there. Traditionalists are very vulnerable to change. Being negatively affected, they typically have difficulty acquiring the necessary skills. Their resistance reflects their underlying insecurity and sense of inadequacy. It is this insecurity and inadequacy that must be addressed head on in

43

their new compacts. Traditionalists are not the risk takers who make up the ranks of change agents, nor are they among the bystanders who can easily acquire the skills and be swayed by the logic of the change effort. As part of their new compacts, they need much more direct help than bystanders.

DESIGNING A NEW COMPACT FRAMEWORK FOR TRADITIONALISTS

The design of traditionalist compacts requires reaching all the way down through the organization to the front-line employees and supervisors, where many traditionalists reside. The big challenge is to make the new compacts so attractive that people throughout the organization are willing to suffer the pain of giving up their old habits as part of fully accepting the new roles required by the change effort. Figure 4.1 shows the managerial challenges involved in designing traditionalist compacts.

Economic dimension	Find the right roles for traditionalists within a comprehensive organizational framework, with the right individual training and support for new skill acquisition
Social dimension	Find the right balance between facilitating individual change and insisting on unequivocal commitment to the change effort

Figure 4.1 Managerial challenges in designing traditionalist compacts

The economic dimension of the new compacts for traditionalists must go beyond the value-creating logic that appeals to bystanders. To give traditionalists a sense of security and the possibility of learning directly from the experience of others, the economic dimension has to be translated into concrete form. Figure 4.2 shows compact features that appeal to traditionalists.

Economic dimension	An organization that is working, with new teams, concrete tasks, training and support, measurement and reward systems
Social dimension	Organizational space and time for adaptation, rules that facilitate direct learning from the change agents and converted bystanders

Figure 4.2 Compact features that appeal to traditionalists

To see how to design attractive compacts for traditionalists, let's look at what John Reeve's team did to bring the traditionalist sales staff on board while Sun Life re-engineered its relationship with its brokers.

Success stories to support the change

(What am I supposed to do?)

Disseminating new organizational success stories is one concrete way for management to provide traditionalists with the living examples (models) they need in order to design their new compacts. Success stories capture the new organizational roles, and can therefore serve as 'concrete' expressions of what employees are supposed to do. Naturally, the new roles present the traditionalists with new tasks, which will, in effect, confront them with the gaps between what they can now do, and what they will be expected to. For traditionalists, facing this gap is commensurate with facing their personal inadequacies. So, the new roles create a demand for training in new skills. As they acquire new work habits and expertise, the traditionalists come to terms with their new environment, and redesign their compacts.

Over the nine weeks that the pilot projects lasted at Sun Life, concrete examples of new relationships formed between the pilot case managers and the brokers. Most of the pilot case managers were meeting customers or brokers face to face for the very first time. In the process, they fleshed out and refined the tasks of the future Sun Life case manager, which gave substance to the new economic com-

45

pact. Many of the apparent worries of the traditionalist sales people and brokers were addressed – especially when the pilot case managers cut the basic processing time for broker requests from 52 to 20 days.

Basic skills training as a vehicle for compact design
(What help will I get?)

Traditionalists usually need nuts and bolts, skills-oriented training. They don't need workshops and discussion groups, which are more appropriate for bystanders. The best foundation for the nuts and bolts training is to systematize the lessons learned during pilot projects and experiments. By providing the basis for the nuts and bolts training, this systematization of the 'learning experiences' also accelerates the roll-out of the new organization. Instead of learning by trial and error on the new job, which would merely increase the perceived risk of the change, traditionalists should be able to design their new compacts based on the experience of the change agents and bystanders.

Sun Life appointed full-time training officers to support the case manager teams. Before taking on their new assignments, future case managers attended a two-week training programme, which was based, in part, on the guide to the new economic compacts documented during the pilot projects. The company created forms and tools to facilitate and simplify the case managers' tasks. They also employed a new accreditation system to monitor how quickly the new case managers picked up their new skills. With the new system, there was no need to check everybody's work, which meant that the training officers could use their time to identify skill gaps.

The training programme included visits to customers and brokers so that the case managers could understand customer needs directly and develop relationships with some brokers. To keep the salespeople and brokers informed when the case managers dealt directly with customers, new 'event logs' tracked what happened during these visits. The event logs not only reassured the sales staff and brokers that the case managers were not undermining their relationships with customers, but equally importantly, they provided the sales staff and brokers with live documentation. The comprehensive nature of the training programme gave the future case managers a complete, non-threatening environment in which they could begin to design much of the economic and social dimensions of their compacts.

Predictable reward and remuneration to reinforce new compacts
(How will I be measured and rewarded?)

Traditionalists are much less willing than change agents and bystanders to assume that they will be remunerated in a manner commensurate with their new tasks and with the effort that they put into the change. Traditionalists want predictability. To get the traditionalists fully behind the change effort, you have to redesign the reward and compensation system explicitly to reinforce the new compacts you have in mind. For traditionalists, this is often the litmus test of whether or not you are sincere about the change; or whether, perhaps, management is just trying to make its life easier, with little real concern for the employees' interests.

At Sun Life, performance measures encouraged the case managers to get into their new roles as quickly as possible. Where possible, Reeve employed 'objective, hard measures of output.' Year-end bonuses were calculated using the revenue account managed by each team, transaction turnover, service quality, and a cost ceiling based on the number of policies processed. What was the advantage of these hard performance measures? They ensured that the new customer service approach led to the economic value creation which had motivated the change in the first place. In addition, a new performance management system rewarded customer service personnel according to three criteria:

- skills acquisition
- effectiveness as an individual and member of a team
- new behaviour.

Quarterly appraisals got case managers and support team members to assess each other's performance. Performing to these metrics meant that the traditionalists had little choice but to design new compacts that supported the change effort.

Tried and tested rules of the game

(What values will I share? and What informal rules will apply?)

To make sure that the new informal rules of the game reinforced Sun Life's new customer-oriented, personal compacts, case manager teams attended quarterly reviews. At these meetings, the case managers presented interim results, performance against targets, turnaround times, and so on, including a 'grumble index' of complaints from customers and brokers. The latter told the teams more about what the customers really wanted and, thereby, kept communication open and maintained the momentum for change. A continuing series of workshops addressed staff concerns, missions, roles, and responsibilities. In addition, top management demonstrated its commitment to open communication and ongoing change in general staff meetings, known as 'Question Time', where people could raise any questions they wanted.

By the time the mass of traditionalists had to respond, the new approach to clients was not merely working – performance had improved dramatically. The details of the new economic compact were clear. People were already talking about the satisfaction of doing a job well, so customers appreciated it. Comments made by case team leaders bear this out: 'It's good to have responsibility for my customers and know I'm giving good service'; ' I've been to see that broker three times and we have a good working relationship.' Doing a job that was inherently more interesting than the one before also brought psychological rewards: 'The job is very much more interesting, varied and satisfying than it was under the old, functional system.' For most of the traditionalists, adapting to their new roles was easier under these conditions.

THE NEW TRADITIONALIST COMPACT AT SUN LIFE

The overall attraction of the new case manager compacts at Sun Life is easy to see:

Economic dimension

What am I supposed to do?	Service all aspects of the broker and customer relationships
What help will I get?	Cross-skilled team members, training, new systems and tools
How will I be measured?	Customer service and team performance measures
What rewards will I get?	Individual performance plus sharing in the team bonus

Social dimension

What vision will I share?	To be number one in the broker market with best customer service
What values will I share?	A new customer orientation and performance-based ethic
What informal rules will apply?	Hierarchy replaced by horizontal teamwork

Psychological dimension

How good is it for me?	Career opportunity, provided I can learn new skills
How risky is it for me?	New tasks, but with full-time training support
What personal satisfaction will I get?	More interesting job, team control over own destiny

The change leaders could not offer everyone such an attractive compact. For some managers in the previous hierarchy, the new organization was a demotion. Rather than directing others, they now had to act as training officers, technical advisors, or facilitators in a support role for customer service. They became resistors. However, with the pilot projects having shown the advantages of integrated customer service, management was determined to implement: 'To move ahead, you don't say anything, you just do it – roll out the new approach, then go back to the brokers and measure the results. We used to worry a lot about staff morale. We stopped worrying and people got used to it.' Once the new organization was in place, those who didn't like it had to buy in anyway. Or leave.

HELPING TRADITIONALISTS COMMIT

You may need to help traditionalists at several points in the process of compact design and commitment :

- *Traditionalist problems should be surfaced early on.* Like the other change response types, traditionalists are generally put off by the announcement of change. They may try to avoid the change by doing something else, like working harder than ever, which lifts their morale temporarily. For example, at Sun Life, the sales staff and brokers claimed they needed to maintain contact, rather than hand their problems over to the case service mangers. As soon as this kind of behaviour appears, you have to find out what's behind it and correct it. Is it a matter of skills, which demand special training, or aptitude, or compensation? Or a matter of habit, as at Sun Life?

- *Functioning new economic compacts should be offered to traditionalists as soon as possible.* When they realize that the change effort is serious, traditionalists try to hide, or escape, convincing themselves that the change is not their concern. To pre-empt this response, you have to put new, workable economic compacts on the table. Traditionalists need success stories and concrete examples that show what's involved *in practice* and what's in it for the individual. If you have not demonstrated with pilot projects (or by other means) that new compacts actually function and that the training, support, and compensation needed for meaningful compact renewal are available, you cannot expect to move traditionalists,

- *You must ask traditionalists to buy in.* On failing to escape the change, traditionalists may become nervous. If this happens, you have to show them they can do it, by putting them into the new organization with skills training. It may also be necessary to wake them up, by burning bridges so they can see there is no way back. Typically, this means dismantling the old organization and processes, and asking the traditionalists to commit as team members to the action plans of the new organization.

Out of 3400 direct staff members at Sun Life, about 1200 went to work in Customer Service and 900 became case managers. But, management clearly could not take the buy-in of traditionalists for granted. To confirm buy-in, management asked the various players and teams to develop their own 'mission statements' and put together action plans. Thus, team leaders, training officers and technical advisors designed action plans that were linked to the corporate vision statement. The agreement on these action plans by the full teams gave management explicit assurance that even the demoted individuals were fully committed.

The results suggest that Sun Life's change process was highly successful in moving a large number of traditionalists into proactive, customer-oriented teams. The turnaround time on administrative transactions dropped by 60 per cent, with 80 per cent fewer process errors. Overhead costs sank by 20 per cent, and unit costs in selling and servicing by 30 per cent. By 1994, Sun Life had climbed to the number one position in the UK broker market, and had jumped from 11th to 4th place in the life and pension market. In 1992 and 1993, it was rated as the 'best performing insurance company in Europe'. The ultimate key to making the change happen throughout the company was getting the traditionalists to renew their compacts, involving them in a new organizational reality – providing tailored training and support, reward and remuneration – as part of a process that explicitly sought their individual commitment.

CONFRONTING RESISTORS WITH MOMENTS OF TRUTH

LJUBLJANSKA BANKA: THE DANGER OF NOT FACING UP TO RESISTORS

Marko Voljc arrived in Ljubljana in 1992 as the new chief executive of the Ljubljanska Banka. He'd been led to expect active support, but he faced active resistance to change above and below.

> 'The people I inherited were either trying to cover their own tracks or run their own fiefdoms within the bank. The two people appointed by the Bank of Slovenia were gaining more authority. The external environment was quite hostile, not just those who associated Ljubljanska Banka with the old socialist regime, but also people I thought would be my allies in the Ministry of Finance and the Bank of Slovenia. They were being very cautious so as not to be perceived as favouring me or the bank during a very tense period.'

Voljc learned the hard way that resistors are acutely aware of what a change effort is all about. And they don't like it. Voljc's experience was the same as that of managers elsewhere. Resistors see change as a threat to their position, power, and interests. They're activists, and they'll do all they can to block change. They may be change agents on existing initiatives, who do not want the current change initiative upsetting their plans. This was the case with the public officials in Slovenia, who didn't want the biggest bank in the country becoming too proactive and upsetting their economic agenda. Alternatively, resistors may be in existing positions of power threatened by the change, unable to see how they can adapt and avoid losing out; to them, resistance means professional survival. This was the case for all the senior executives in Ljubljanska Banka.

Resistors quickly learn to exploit the political system of a company. They use the informal rules of current play to turn as many bystanders and traditionalists as possible against renewing their personal compacts. If they succeed in their political power game, they not only block change; they turn the tables against the change leadership and the change agents, putting them into the position of resistors, forcing them to accept the status quo.

After taking the first steps to put Ljubljanska Banka back on track to financial health, Voljc left for a short break in the summer of 1993, and things took a turn for the worse. The Bank of Slovenia, which had been tightening monetary policy to fight inflation, virtually ran out of liquidity to lend to Ljubljanska Banka. The interbank market rate jumped to 18–20 per cent above inflation; Ljubljanska tumbled into a liquidity crisis. At the same time, the two top executives appointed by the Bank of Slovenia began circulating a rumour that the Bank of Slovenia believed that Voljc had failed in his task and was on his way out. On hearing about this, Voljc rushed back to Ljubljana.

To force resistors to show their hand, you have to confront them with a moment of truth. You have to lay out your view of the change in an unequivocal way – you have to constrain them to commit, or take the consequences.

TACTICS FOR CONFRONTING RESISTORS WITH MOMENTS OF TRUTH

Depending on the pressure you are under, you can be more or less subtle about dealing with resistors. In many cases, time pressure will force you to remove resistors quickly. Many managers, with hindsight, say they should have acted faster. In other cases, the distribution of power is more complicated. This was the case at Ljubljanska Banka.

Sandwiching the resistors with change agents

Although the pressure was mounting on Ljubljanska Banka, Marko Voljc knew that the public authorities could not afford to let Ljubljanska fail, so he had time for a step-by-step approach. To deal with the resistors, to build credibility and acceptance, he had to build a constituency inside the bank. He adopted what he called a 'parallel systems' approach. Voljc began to put his own change management team in place, positioning outside people above the official management group and putting a team of change agents below them. By putting the top management resistors in a 'sandwich' of his own people, Voljc effectively squeezed the resistors between two layers of change agents.

Voljc extended his 'parallel systems' approach to deal with the bank's technical problems. He hand-picked people to work on problems that would nominally have been the responsibility of others in the bank. One of the most important was determining the bank's cash flow, by department. Voljc selected 30 staff members from various departments to work on the cash flow project. Once they started getting an idea of where the money was going, many of their bosses started getting scared and attempted to block the group's efforts, by preventing their subordinates from attending the team meetings. According to Safi Harb, the International Finance Corporation advisor on Voljc's change leadership team, 'Within 10 days it became clear which bosses were helpful and which weren't. Out of 30 managers, only four turned out to be reliable.' With the parallel teams, Voljc could address pressing technical issues, and at the same time, identify and pressure the resistors.

Making the economic dimension of the new compact explicit

To draw people's attention to the need for compact renewal and further pin down the resistors, Voljc organized a retreat for the bank's 40 middle and upper level managers: 'I wanted to get a better feel for what people's expectations and willingness to contribute were, while at the same time removing some of the divisional monopolies held by top managers.' Harb started the meeting with a 'wake-up call' – he publicly told each vice-president and director where he or she had failed. Harb didn't even spare Voljc. After the wake-up call, Harb left the meeting.

Managerial presentations were next on the agenda. Each manager started with a response to Harb's critique in front of the group and then presented a report covering four topics:

- an explanation of his department's function
- his own positive contributions to the bank
- ideas about how he could be more effective
- a list of the ways he could improve himself.

These presentations got the managers to begin redesigning the economic dimension of their compacts. In the afternoon, the group split into workshops to cover technical issues. The evening and the second day were devoted to social and sporting activities to calm nerves and bring people together again. According to one of Voljc's younger executives, 'the first retreat was a landmark in the sense that the issues weren't dealt with in a conference room in one hour, after which everyone was dismissed. People realized they were part of a team.' Nevertheless, Voljc estimated they had convinced only about 10 per cent of the managers.

The relative success of the retreat, as well as Voljc's ability to improve the liquidity situation (by halting all lending except to AAA clients, cutting costs, divesting non-bankable assets, borrowing money from bank subsidiaries abroad, and getting the Bank of Slovenia temporarily to reduce the reserve requirements for Ljubljanska) strengthened Voljc's position *vis à vis* the top resistors.

Breaking down the power base of resistors

To undermine further the position of the resistors, Voljc broke down the bank's fiefdoms with additional project teams made up of middle managers. Using the strategic priorities that emerged from the first retreat, Voljc formed 18 multi-divisional project groups, composed of four to five members. Each focused on a particular issue confronting the bank. The timing of the project groups coincided with the arrival of consultants from the Allied Irish Bank, with which Ljubljanska had set up a 'twinning arrangement' supported by the European Community. The Irish consultants teamed up separately with the project groups to provide hands-on advice on various technical issues, and supplemental training followed in Dublin.

Voljc saw that 'all of a sudden project work became prestigious, and everyone wanted to do it'. In effect, the project work gave a significant number of middle manager change agents and bystanders a chance to renew their compacts. The project groups had free rein to complete their tasks, with only occasional meetings with Voljc's steering committee. When a project group finished its work, it would present a report to top management and, in many cases, to the Bank Rehabilitation Agency. Top management would then issue a directive to the organization about the new procedure.

The combination of upward pressure from the project groups and top-down pressure from Voljc, plus his much improved relationship with the Bank of Slovenia, finally had the desired effect on the resistors at the very top. Voljc felt he had the leverage to confront the two problematic executives who had been put in place originally by the Bank of Slovenia. He gave them the choice of accepting a new compact, or leaving. After a second management retreat confirmed Voljc's support, the two left (with some other resistors lower down). Voljc then reorganized the bank, consolidating the previous six divisions into three.

DESIGNING A COMPACT TO CONVERT RESISTORS

If resistors can be converted, like all new converts they can sometimes be among the most enthusiastic and energetic supporters of the change effort. Their very resistance shows that they understand what the stakes are, and they have the energy to do something about it. The challenge is to try to redirect this energy. To do so requires time, the time to try to understand why the resistors refuse to renew their compacts, and what can be done to encourage them to do so.

The question is whether a way can be found to get resistors to begin to redesign and align the economic dimension of their compacts with the change effort. Often, you merely have to provide the right channel and support for their involvement by designing the new compact framework so realistic activists can embrace it. Figure 5.1 shows compact features that appeal to resistors.

Economic dimension	The choice between a viable role in a successful change effort, or leaving the company
Social dimension	No recrimination for having been a resistor, but rules making it clear that covert resistance will not be tolerated
Psychological dimension	A meaningful role to offset wounded pride and save face on shifting position to join the change

Figure 5.1 Compact features that appeal to resistors

You have to decide whether there is enough time – and the resistor competencies worth the effort – to help them commit. If not, power must be deployed to force the resistors out. The challenges in compacts designed for the resistors you help are summarized in Figure 5.2.

Economic dimension	Finding a role that capitalizes on the strength of the resistors without destabilizing the rest of the change effort
Social dimension	Getting resistors to accept unequivocally new formal rules of the game that crowd out the old informal rules they prefer

Figure 5.2 Managerial challenges in designing resistor compacts

HELPING RESISTORS COMMIT

To help resistors commit, you have to be sensitive to the emotional voyage they take when they convert to the change effort. Being actively against the change, resistors have to alter their behaviour more than the other players do – they ride a wilder 'roller coaster' of morale. They have to give up activities and/or roles that they value deeply as part of their self identity, accept the loss, and then go on to something new. You can help resistors with the process of individual commitment in several ways.

- *Get the economic dimension right, so resistors do not think that resistance can succeed.* Resistors often try to offset the first news of change by accusing the change leaders of disrupting the business. If possible, they will cast you as a scapegoat for the poor business per- formance that has made the change necessary. You had better be right about what you are trying to do, with a strong enough value- creating idea to offer resistors attractive new personal compacts, especially on the economic dimension, so that they can get involved in a constructive way. At Ljubljanska Banka, the value-creating ideas driving change in the early days of Voljc's tenure were too weak to prevent the resistors from building some support.
- *Get the social dimension right, so you can offer resistors a mean- ingful role, provided they fully commit to the change.* In some cases, the resistance is in large part psychological – that someone else is taking the lead and that they have not been given the role they expect can be a blow to the ego and cause wounded pride. So it should come as no surprise that resistors are liable to try to sabo- tage the change. When they realize that the change effort is serious, they may vent their frustration by using the formal and informal rules of the game to fight the change. Before giving resistors roles in the change process, therefore, you have to be confident that the rules of the game, particularly the informal rules, are consistent enough with the change effort to take away any temptation resis-

tors may have to try to undermine the change effort from within.

- *Confront the resistors with the choice of buying in, or leaving.* As their fight to block the change fails, resistors become frustrated and, to hang on to the status quo, may resort to irrational behaviour. In the face of the commotion, you have to be cool and firm. At this point, you have to confront the resistors with a clear choice: either commit to a new compact, or leave. In many cases, as the Ljubljanska Banka story illustrates, the resistors realize that their strengths and abilities are not what is needed. To convert them, find roles and new compacts that take advantage of their strengths; otherwise, ask them to leave.

GETTING THE COMMITMENT OF RESISTORS AT
LJUBLJANSKA BANKA

To signal that the reorganization also meant a new way of working, Voljc and his right-hand man asked for a formal commitment from the top 40 or so managers.

> 'We spoke to the top 40 or so managers and offered them jobs in the new structure with new written contracts. Each member of the top management team then had an *explicit and implicit contract* with all the other managers in the top three layers of management.'

The new contracts offered managers higher wages and improved benefits, such as life insurance. In return, managers had to make a stronger commitment to the bank; those who wouldn't had no choice but to leave.

Structurally, the reorganization was a series of steps. To allow learning to occur before imposing changes on the entire organization, pilot projects preceded many of the changes. For the traditionalists who wanted training to help them adapt to the changes more easily, Voljc initiated a series of communication and other tailor-made seminars.

On 27 July 1994, in a special session, the Slovenian parliament split the Ljubljanska Banka into two parts. In one part, the shell company, the government put all the liabilities that were out of management's control (the State of Slovenia agreed to assume claims by foreign creditors on these debts). The rest of the bank got the name Nova Ljubljanska Banka and took over the bulk of the previous operations and staff. Together with the reorganization mentioned above, this financial restructuring essentially completed the transition to a profitable, market-oriented bank.

After two more retreats at Ljubljanska Banka, very few active resistors were left. The remaining challenges began to sound more and more like those of any bank trying to grapple with the changes in the financial services industry:

- How can we sustain change?
- How can we get people on the front-line to become more market-oriented?
- What is the right balance for us between retail, wholesale, investment banking, and other financial services?

By mid-1995, Voljc could report that the bank's profit picture was so good that public officials were beginning to comment enviously on its resources. With a deliberate and explicit approach to the resistors, Voljc had turned a delicate situation around.

Converting resistors can be rewarding. But it can also backfire if the resistors sense that they can turn the clock back by influencing bystanders and traditionalists to resist the process of getting front-line commitment. To prevent this from happening, you must have sufficient power to intervene in the process and keep it on track, which, as we shall see in the next chapter, means having a viable compact with *your* boss.

DESIGNING A
CHANGE LEADERSHIP
COMPACT

SPAARBELEG: CHANGE LEADERSHIP COMPACT WITH THE MANAGEMENT BOARD

'You are being sent to Elba!' was what Johan van der Werf's colleagues said when he was appointed managing director of Spaarbeleg, the struggling retail investment products division of Aegon, the large Dutch insurance company. However, van der Werf got almost complete freedom from the Management Board of Aegon to try and turn the division around. They agreed to measure his performance simply in terms of Spaarbeleg's performance. If he succeeded, he could look forward to a further promotion. As a sign of their support, the Management Board agreed to put off the projected move of the division to The Hague, to give van der Werf the psychological leverage he believed was necessary to mobilize his people and deal with the change politics.

Few change leaders are as farsighted as van der Werf. Blinded by the challenge of leading change and designing new relationships, they overlook the necessity of developing a compact with their superiors to ensure that both sides agree on the terms of the assignment. And then at a crucial moment, when the change process needs it most, support from upstairs is lukewarm, or not forthcoming. The change effort fails and the change leader takes the blame. As a change leader, beyond making sure you have a good compact with your peers and subordinates, especially the change leadership team, you have to ensure that you have a robust leadership compact with your boss. Getting the compacts at the top right is crucial to designing a viable set of new compacts.

DESIGNING THE ECONOMIC AND SOCIAL DIMENSIONS OF A LEADERSHIP COMPACT

The right balance between taking advantage of your own style and adapting to the change context is at the heart of the design of a viable leadership compact. Certain dimensions of the compact should fit your style; other dimensions should fit the context of change.

Economic dimension of change leader's compact: select a role that plays to your strengths

In today's competitive environment, you can only add economic value to the change process and the business if you play to your strengths. To try to adapt to the change context at the expense of your strengths typically backfires. If your strengths are not what the change process needs, it is better to refuse an active leadership role, and instead take on a supporting role, acting as a sponsor or facilitator. Either way, a clear personal compact with your immediate superiors should reinforce your chosen role.

When you redesign your compact with your superiors, the face-to-face dialogue should cover the following issues:

Leadership compact: economic dimension

What am I going to do?	Clear objectives, duration of mandate
What help will I get?	The power and freedom to act, plus resources
How will I be measured?	Agreement on performance criteria, risk distribution
What rewards will I get?	Understanding about benefits if the change is successful

Social dimension of change leader's compact: emphasize your values and accommodate team members who fit change needs

For the leadership team to be effective, your boss and the members of the team must share your values. And these must be values that you believe in. With common values as the centre-piece, what matters is the social dimension of your compact, not so much with your superiors as with your team members. To bring the latter on board, it is essential to create formal and informal rules of the game that can accommodate other players on the change leadership team, whose competence and natural style fit what the change process needs.

Leadership compact: social dimension

What vision and values will I share with others?	The things that are central to my view of the world and how I want to manage the change process
What informal rules of behaviour will apply?	Those that reflect my natural management style and can accommodate other players with appropriate competence.

FINDING THE RIGHT MEMBERS OF THE LEADERSHIP TEAM

Finding potential team members who fit your values and satisfy the change needs is not straightforward. To find the right people, you have to expose them to the need for change and evaluate their response. This can be done in several basic ways. You can, for example:

- build scenarios to communicate the potential impact of the change force
- expose people directly to the change force
- use shock to dramatize the impact of the change force.

With the construction of challenging scenarios, you can judge whether people will fit into the leadership team. In effect, scenarios dare people to consider what would happen if certain extreme situations actually come to pass. They raise the question of what would be required to ensure that the company could deal with the situation. Equally important, scenarios give you the opportunity to highlight the values you believe in. And this gives people the opportunity to imagine what their new compacts will be like if they join the change leadership team.

A very effective way of judging whether people will fit into the change leadership team is to expose them personally to the change force, in the form of a customer, competitor, or internal change agent. Such person-to-person contact works not only intellectually, but also emotionally, through the heart and gut. Rather than trying to convince others about the need for change, you let them feel it for themselves. For example, bench-marking against competitors – not only by collecting data, but by visiting competitive facilities – gives people the real context in which they will have to redesign their compacts to join the change team.

Finally, if the present organizational set-up prevents you from exposing people personally to the change forces, you may have to use shock treatment, or some defining event, to reposition the organization so that people can see and feel the change forces, and potential members of the change leadership team can show their hand.

A DEFINING EVENT AT SPAARBELEG TO FIND THE RIGHT TEAM MEMBERS

At Spaarbeleg, van der Werf had difficulty getting people to be enthusiastic about increasing sales. They didn't see how it could be done. But van der Werf was determined to coach and cajole the Spaarbeleg people into coming up with the sales and new products that Spaarbeleg needed. After many attempts to convince them individually, he decided to change tactics. He called a meeting in a small room to discuss the product range. Once there, he refused to let anyone leave until they had come up with a joint approach to Spaarbeleg's problem. 'It was tough and painful, many people were sweating ... Yes, we came up with a new product, but it was really emotion and energy and drama.' The meeting gave van der Werf the chance to see who could work with him on his team. So strong were the emotions raised that those who felt uncomfortable left soon thereafter. These included the sales manager and several others.

After the defining meeting at Spaarbeleg, van der Werf was in a position to hand-pick his team. He went to Madrid to interview the future Manager of Information Systems and Finance. According to the latter, van der Werf:

'suggested that we meet at my house, with my wife present and the children running in and out. I remember that afternoon very clearly; we talked about the marketing approach, customer values, products, but also about problems and internal weaknesses at Spaarbeleg. And it was not just business, but real life! We got into many personal issues, not just his questioning me, but in both directions.'

This very personal approach was part of van der Werf's value system. He made sure that all new recruits to the management team spent a lot of time with the existing team members 'to see if they fit our values, if they are open to learn, if they smell right'.

LINKING THE COMPACTS OF THE LEAD TEAM MEMBERS TO THE CHANGE LEADER

The key to the economic dimension is the clarity of each member's compact with the leader, which should cover points similar to those mentioned in the change leader's compact (outlined above). Real teams are characterized by joint work and joint output rather than the combination of individual outputs so common in working groups. The members of real teams also help one another learn, thereby providing self-development for each of the team members. Thus, on the economic dimension, the compact design dialogue should cover the following:

Team members' compact: economic dimension

What am I going to do?	Define role relative to others and commit to the team effort
How will I be measured?	Collective and individual targets, milestones, and responsibilities

| *What help will I get?* | Working methods, values, mutual help, conflict resolution |
| *What rewards will I get?* | Self-development, team-work, accomplishing team's mandate |

On the social dimension, the core of the lead team members' compact is the bond of trust with the change leader:

Team members' compact: social dimension

| *What vision and values will I share with others?* | A new economic value-creating idea, same personal values as the change leader |
| *What informal rules of behaviour will apply?* | Rules of behaviour supporting the implementation of the value-creating idea and consistent with our values. |

LEAD TEAM MEMBERS' COMPACT AT SPAARBELEG

At Spaarbeleg, van der Werf created a leadership compact that led to a real team of change managers.

Economic dimension

Van der Werf set challenging targets that drove the business team work. The idea of developing savings products linked to the performance of the stockmarket opened up new opportunities that no one in the Netherlands had yet tapped. In order to reach a much larger mass consumer market with their new products, the team added telephone, advertising, and direct mail channels to the existing broker channel. In addition, they redesigned the information systems to provide more rapid feedback on customer needs and how new products were doing.

The change in the behaviour of the management team set the tone for the rest of the organization. Van der Werf set very ambitious performance targets; pursuing them required redesigning the unit's entire business system. This didn't just mean new processes. It meant taking a new, more profit-oriented, customer-sensitive approach, based on a new way of working together, a new set of organizational habits: more analytical and merit-oriented, with a strong group orientation, and with recognition and money being important.

Social dimension

Van der Werf put a lot of emphasis on the social dimension. He was continually 'walking the talk' in management meetings and one-to-one meetings with each of the managers. He insisted that team members buy into his values. The balance between risk and commitment was one of the things that van der Werf was most concerned about. He was insistent on the link between the willingness to take risk and commitment. 'Consensus is about sharing risk. Commitment is about taking risk. Consensus is in the head. Commitment comes from the stomach.'

To commit emotionally and take the risk to support change, the team members have to trust you. To get that trust, you not only have to be credible, you in turn have to trust your people. In the words of van der Werf, 'I have discovered that if you really rely on people, eight out of ten things they do will be right, and they'll enjoy it. So I help them build the concept, then they build what has to be done ... Even if they make mistakes, they learn that it is OK, they can correct it'. According to members of the Spaarbeleg team, van der Werf's emotional commitment was an integral part of their commitment to him.

The Dutch preference for direct, relatively informal relations between people on different levels was central in the relations between Johan van der Werf and his team. Van der Werf emphasized participation and personal development in teams throughout the organization. His compacts were based on intensive interaction to provide the maximum opportunity for self-development and sincerity, what van der Werf called the difference between the 'real and unreal'.

> 'Once we understand the strategy and vision, I tell them "you decide what you want to do that's your part of the company"... If a person stops learning, stops really experiencing new things, they fall out, they can't contribute to the work of the company... Real and unreal refers to being true to yourself, being real in yourself, not having a facade or being fake.'

Needless to say, not everyone found the intensity of van der Werf's new compacts attractive. People could not be indifferent. They had to buy into his vision and style, or go.

Another key element at Spaarbeleg

Anticipating the discussion in Part III of this book, another key element of van der Werf's approach was a continual review of the value-creating idea and how people could contribute to it. According to one of them, 'We talk about my people, what we are experiencing, and a lot about what's important to me ... Conceptually, his vision is clear; he stays out of operational issues and gets us to think about what we are really trying to do.' Occasionally, this leads to a reevaluation of the compact. 'It requires you to be capable of asking: Who am I? What can I do? What can I really contribute and what can I learn from others' contributions?' Such ongoing compact renewal was an important factor in the commitment of the management team, spurring Spaarbeleg to dramatic profit improvements of more than 300 per cent during the first five years of the nineties. This, in a slow growth industry environment, with the same number of personnel as when van der Werf joined the division.

Notwithstanding van der Werf's particular style, change leaders of all types are unanimous on this point: a viable leadership compact is essential for a successful change effort. Whereas some people can be lucky enough to succeed without a clear compact with their superiors, all agree that a viable compact within the leadership team is critical.

Once you have a viable leadership compact and have designed the compact framework for the other players, as described in the previous chapters, you are ready actually to orchestrate compact renewal throughout the organization. Part II will show you how.

Part II

ORCHESTRATING COMPACT RENEWAL

The second step towards compacts for ongoing change, is to get people to buy into the initial compact framework. To do so, you have to orchestrate compact renewal in a way that takes account of the change context. This involves putting together a change process that gives the various players, successively, the opportunity to renew their compacts and buy in. Chapter 7 shows you how to choose the right compact renewal process for each of four classic contexts. Chapters 8 to 11 then describe the best tactics and sequence of compact renewal for each of these change processes, while Chapter 12 shows you how to deal with the accompanying politics.

CHOOSING
THE RIGHT PROCESS
FOR COMPACT
RENEWAL

DIFFERENT SITUATIONS DEMAND DIFFERENT PROCESSES

'This is the second time we've gone for front-line initiative to get growth. We rolled out task force recommendations to all the business unit managers, set targets and milestones, but nothing is really happening,' exclaimed the CEO of a large services company to his senior managers, the edge in his voice betraying his rising frustration. After an embarrassing silence, one of his colleagues on the management committee said, 'We've never really had an entrepreneurial culture, Rainer. Our people are used to going upstairs for approval of every new move. We've got to convince them that they can take reasonable risks without getting their heads chopped off'.

Executives who call for growth and entrepreneurship compacts from the top down in tightly run organizations inevitably suffer the frustration of poor or non-existent results. It is impossible for people on the front line to take the risk in entrepreneurial compacts without the necessary organizational space to do so. Conversely, executives who call for cost discipline from the bottom up in a decentralized organization inevitably discover that they have no choice but to act top-down. It is very difficult for middle managers to design new compacts based on cost cutting, if those around them are going off in different directions. In short, if the wrong change process is adopted, it becomes impossible to control the risk associated with compact renewal.

To get people to take up your offer of a new compact framework and actually renew their compacts, you need a process that fits the business situation. Different situations demand different change processes, different approaches to the orchestration of compact renewal. Those who pretend that the same medicine can be applied no matter what the context, completely miss the variety of possible change processes and corresponding approaches to compact renewal. A situation in which turnaround management makes sense is quite different from that in which widespread participation might be appropriate. And the orchestration of compact renewal for turnaround is quite different from that which makes sense for widespread participation. As a change leader, you cannot afford to risk blindly applying a standard change recipe, hoping that people on the front line will automatically manage the risk and renew their compacts.

CHOOSING THE RIGHT CHANGE PROCESS

The choice of the right change process for the orchestration of front-line commitment depends, first, on the pressure for change created by the external change force, that is, the intensity of the threat to the business, or the opportunity it faces. The right change process depends, second, on the strength of the resistance to change, that is, how open or closed the organization is to the change. You can use two questions to assess the strength of these forces:

- To assess the strength of the change force, ask: *how intense are the external forces and how clear is their direction in terms of the threat to the company, or alternatively, the size of the opportunity?*

  The strength of the change force is determined by its impact on the company's performance (most frequently measured by market share, sales, or profits). A strong change force can either cause a substantial decline in the performance of a company under threat, or promise a substantial improvement in the performance of a company with an opportunity.

- To assess the strength of the resistance, ask: *how open are the company's internal and external stakeholders to the implications of the forces of change?*

  This question reflects the mix of individual responses to the change. Resistors and traditionalists dominate in organizations that are closed to change, whereas change agents are influential in open organizations.

These two dimensions of change force intensity and organizational resistance provide a simple framework for choosing the right change process. The combinations of low/high change force intensity and organizational resistance correspond to four classic change processes, which are shown in Figure 7.1.

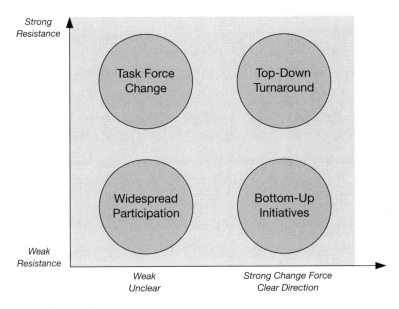

Figure 7.1 The basic change processes

The intensity of the change force determines how much time is available and the clarity of the change direction. Strong change forces demand a rapid response, to prevent collapse by means of a turnaround in a crisis, or in the other extreme, to capitalize on an opportunity with bottom-up initiatives on the front line. The crisis, or the opportunity as the case may be, generally provides a clear indication of the direction the change must take, making a rapid response possible. By contrast, when the change force is weak, it is typically not clear what direction the change should take. However, more time is available to try to determine the appropriate direction of the change with the help of task forces, or widespread participation.

The degree of resistance shapes the focus of the initiative for compact renewal, whether it has to come from the top, or whether it can be driven from the front line.

IN CLOSED ORGANIZATIONS, COMPACT RENEWAL HAS TO BE DRIVEN FROM THE TOP

In closed organizations, where the resistors and their passive traditionalist allies dominate, you have to generate the energy for compact renewal from the top down. You have to deal with the resistors at the top before any change is possible; ideally, they should be cleared out before you call on the change agents. Once you have communicated the change objectives and change process, you can give others the opportunity to buy in, and you can put in place the change organization, training, and supporting resources to encourage compact renewal.

Top-down turnaround

Intense forces of change on a closed organization demand rapid, radical action by top management if the business is to be saved. Since time is so limited, the change leadership has to prescribe people's compacts and present them almost on a take-it-or-leave-it basis, leaving little room for individual discretion. This is especially true for the resistors who have to be dealt with early on to reduce the risk of their undermining the change effort.

A number of well known change processes fall into the category of top-down turnaround:

- downsizing
- restructuring
- realigning.

When the change force reaches crisis proportions, when it threatens the survival of the business, radical downsizing and restructuring are the only alternatives. The turnaround at Philips, the large Dutch electronics company, in the early nineties, had all the typical characteristics of a radical top-down turnaround.

When Jan Timmer took over as CEO, Philips was close to bankruptcy. Market share had been falling, it had been overtaken by Sony in its home market, and margins had been declining for some time. The company was facing a financial crisis. Yet, the resistance to change, generated by the long years of success after the Second World War, by the not-invented-here syndrome of its strong engineering department, and by the lack of accuracy associated with its standard cost accounting, made the resistance to change enormous. Previous CEOs had identified the problems clearly enough, but had been unable to get any change on the front line. In Chapter 8, we shall see how Timmer managed the situation by introducing what he called new 'personal contracts'.

Task force change

When a closed organization faces an undefined, weak change force, the best approach to compact renewal is with task forces. The uncertainty around the change direction makes it foolhardy to initiate radical change on the hunch of someone at the top. You have to open up the organization with incremental experimentation by off-line task forces. Although the task force members should have discretion in how they will actually work, they must solicit opinions widely, especially from the bystanders. To put the results of the task force into practice, you have to orchestrate compact renewal for the rest of the organization with systematic implementation groups.

Robert Kohl, the chief executive of Medoil, the oil and gas subsidiary of a major German multinational, faced strong resistance to his declared intention of re-engineering the company's production and delivery process. Although profits were still acceptable, Medoil had been experiencing large cost overruns, errors, and safety problems on its off-shore platforms. Unfortunately, earlier initiatives by previous chief executives had petered out, making the men on the platforms especially cynical about change proposals from head-quarters. In addition, the company was plagued by the 'silo effect': the development, construction, and production departments oper-ated completely independently, with very little interaction, making it extremely difficult to implement efficient cross-divisional processes.

Kohl's predecessor had failed on the front line with his top-down turnaround, because good financial results had weakened the urgency needed to get people actually to change their behaviour. The departmental managers, moreover, were at best lukewarm about the turn-around, despite various incentives. The relatively weak change force, plus the strong resistance, made a task force approach the only option. In order to demonstrate the benefits, Kohl simply had to use task forces to redesign the processes and run some experiments based on the new processes. What happened? The resistors immediately obstructed the task forces. Chapter 9 will show how he dealt with the problem.

IN OPEN ORGANIZATIONS, THE FRONT LINE CAN DRIVE COMPACT RENEWAL

In open organizations, you can ask your change agents not only to help develop the value-creating idea, but also to bring the other play-ers on board. In such cases, compact renewal starts with the change agents. Here, the key to success is having an experimental sub-culture to nurture their new compacts. Where such a culture does not exist, you have to take special care in the design of the change compacts for the change agents. However, once you've got them on board, you can 'employ' their commitment to help drive the renewal of the compacts of the other players.

If you're in an open organization, and resistors are not threatening the compact renewal of others, you can leave them to last. You are taking a small risk in waiting to deal with them, because the change effort builds up organically, gradually pervading the organization, before taking it over entirely. As a result, you can let the process take its due course: the resistors will be reduced to a shrinking group of pariahs who have yet to revise their compacts in the face of an accelerating change bandwagon. Those who refuse to join the bandwagon will effectively be isolated right out of the organization. When the change forces are less intense, however, the resistors may begin questioning the direction taken. You must deal with them sooner rather than later.

Widespread participation

When the direction provided by the change forces is unclear, you cannot afford the risk of leaving your change agents alone, because they may strike out in a direction that is incompatible with the long-run strategy of the company. Rather, you have to participate with the front line, discuss the need for change, develop a shared understanding of what has to be done, and a shared commitment to action. Here, your employees negotiate, or participate in setting the mandates and objectives of their compacts.

A participative approach to compact renewal may take longer to initiate than the top-down approach appropriate in more closed organizations, but individual ownership of the new compacts is more complete and the execution of the change effort that much smoother. This is the domain of continued improvement and Total Quality Management.

At Ford of Europe (FOE), widespread participation followed a three-year streamlining effort, driven by taskforces, that had only been partially successful. The taskforce approach had at least opened people up to change by familiarizing them with the underlying issues. On the other hand, FOE's results were still reasonable, so that, as in the case of Medoil, it had been difficult to motivate the streamlining. Murray Reichenstein, the Chief Financial Officer and one of the architects of the effort, realized that compared to its Japanese competitors, Ford was still top heavy and over-controlled.

In Reichenstein's view, to catch up with the Japanese, the next step would have to be more participative, to get everyone involved in setting the objectives for, and implementing, the next round of cost reduction and process improvement. But given Ford's very traditional top-down culture, this was easily said. Not easily done. Getting people to go beyond complaining and participate in taking collective initiative from the bottom up would be a huge challenge. In Chapter 10, we shall see how FOE's top management proceeded.

Bottom-up initiatives

When the change force is strong and the direction clear, you can empower capable people in an open organization to take the initiative on their own, without much guidance from the top. Within the overall strategic and organizational guidelines, employees have full discretion in designing their new personal compacts. Giving them the room to act is often the most effective and rapid way of capitalizing on clear opportunities.

Some American companies – among the most renowned are 3M and Hewlett Packard – have made stimulating continual entrepreneurial activity from the bottom up into a fine art. Although an innovative market offering may draw on a new technology, the key to business success is compacts that encourage the internal entrepreneurship needed to transform the idea or technology into viable products.

At Performance Chemicals, the UK subsidiary of a US multinational, customers out in the field were clamouring for more customization of the chemical additives that Performance was delivering to their drilling sites. But John Norman, the divisional executive, could not get his sales engineers to customize and innovate. As soon as they ran into a problem, or special request, they called on someone from the central laboratories to come out into the field to deal with it. As the requests piled up, the central laboratory was soon overextended and customer dissatisfaction was ballooning.

Time was short. If Norman didn't act quickly, market share would slip rapidly. There was no time for lengthy taskforce experiments, no time for widespread participative change activity. Norman couldn't order the sales engineers to innovate top down. On the positive side, though, having weathered numerous change projects over the years, the sales engineers were very well qualified. At least they knew about change. In Chapter 11, you will see what Norman did, how he orchestrated compact renewal for bottom-up initiatives.

TURNAROUND
COMPACT RENEWAL

PHILIPS: DRAMATIC TAKE-IT-OR-LEAVE APPROACH

Shortly after taking over as CEO of Philips, the Dutch electronics company, Jan Timmer invited the company's top 100 managers to an off-site retreat at the Philips training centre in De Ruwenberg, Holland. He handed out a mock press release stating that Philips was bankrupt. Its survival was at stake. It was up to the managers in the room to bring it back. Operation Centurion, the process Timmer would use to turn Philips around, had begun. He offered his managers new compacts, which were like the assignments given to officers by their superiors in the Roman Army:

> 'Centurion was the rank given to an officer in the Roman Army, who received his assignment in the form of a personal contract. Philips managers, too, will have to handle their personal assignments, that is their budget, as a personal contract. It will mean keeping your word by following through on your promises.'

Timmer's terms for change were tough and unambiguous; those present had no choice but to accept the new compact framework, or prepare their exit.

TURNAROUND APPROACH TO COMPACT RENEWAL

To get compact renewal in the midst of a turnaround, when you are facing a crisis in a closed organization, you have to make sure people understand how serious the situation is, provide a clear new compact framework, and get people to buy in and move into action fast.

Here are the key ingredients and steps in the turnaround approach:

Turnaround approach to compact renewal

Style:	Commander, take-it-or-leave.
Design:	Top-down.

Renewal sequence and tactics:	1. Force resistors out by making buy-in immediate.
	2. Ask change agents to cascade the change down.
	3. Unequivocal message to bystanders.
	4. Rapid reorganization for traditionalists.
Key success factor:	A viable compact for those who stay.
Pitfall:	Hubris of the commander.

COMMANDER STYLE LEADERSHIP COMPACT

Philips was facing a crisis and its organization was closed to change, the classic context for a top-down turnaround. Jan Timmer was the classic commander. In terms of preferred approach to compact renewal, his contracting style was very much that of the decisive leader, offering his people new compacts that they could not easily refuse. People could propose minor adjustments to their compacts but then they had to buy in or walk out. The compact renewal dialogue was dramatic and focused.

From his superiors, Timmer wanted a definite mandate with maximum individual discretion in implementation. The Philips Board gave Timmer what he wanted: the legitimacy and power to demand fundamental shifts in the compacts between the employees, which amounted to giving him his own strong compact to do what had to be done to turn the company around: cut costs and improve the response to customers.

At the first meetings for the top 100 managers, Timmer made it abundantly clear that he would not tolerate resistance to the need for reducing costs. The new personal contracts would be based on a manager's budget, reflecting a promise that Timmer expected each manager to fulfill. This entailed

'calling entrenched views and habits into question, simplifying methods of work and constantly improving quality awareness, customer orientation and cost consciousness ... (which) requires a readiness to be self-critical and to be merciless in comparing ourselves with the best in various sectors, and also the will to bring about improvement.'

No matter what the focus of the turnaround, it invariably divides employees into three distinct categories:

- those who have to leave
- those who move to an outsourcing relationship
- those who stay.

Those who become subcontractors have to make a huge personal shift: their psychological/emotional and social relationship with the company is broken. If they maintain links, in the end, they have a purely economic contract with the company governed by the laws of the market place. Those who are retained as full-time employees have a distinctly different compact, as full-time employees, they have to renew their compacts on all three dimensions. To rebuild their confidence that they will not be the next sacrificial victims in the ongoing dynamics of turnaround, they look for explicit compact terms.

At Philips, Timmer drew a line. He invited those who wanted to stay to make a compact with him to turn the company around. Timmer told his executives that those who could create value would always be in demand. To create turnaround value at Philips, their budgets had to strike a balance between being so ambitious they couldn't be achieved, and so conservative that they didn't represent a challenge. The executives would be solely responsible for the bottom line of their units. They had to calculate the risk of new initiatives, for there would be no excuses when things went sour. Major investments, or the launch of a new product, had to be supported by the cash flow of the unit. From now on, managers had to do the best they could with the resources they could find, additional resources being negotiated only when yearly plans and budgets were decided.

SEQUENCE AND TACTICS FOR TURNAROUND COMPACT RENEWAL

In organizations facing a crisis, no change is possible until you have dealt with the resistance that led to the crisis. Remember: few people will be neutral about the need for change. Most people will be change agents or resistors, depending on the value-creating idea selected to get out of the crisis. The sequence of compact renewal, beyond the change team, has to start with the resistors at the top. Ideally, you should ask the resistors to leave, even before you seek the support of the change agents. Thereafter, you can communicate the change objectives and ask the bystanders to join the change agents in implementation. You can then deploy change organization, training, and other resources to roll out the change and bring the traditionalists on board.

Force resistors out by making buy-in explicit

At Philips, Timmer gave the resistors no room to manoeuvre. The first big meeting of the top 100 did not end until each of the divisions had accepted new compacts, in an oral agreement with Timmer on their target head count reduction and operating costs. Personal compact design started with discussion of the detail on the economic dimension of the new compacts. Timmer asked each manager what he could contribute to the lowering operating costs through an initial 10 per cent reduction in the work force (later the figure would be hitched up to 20 per cent). The meeting broke into sub-groups to allow each division to consider its response, and, in the process, allocate targets (including work force reductions) to each of the business unit managers. Thus, managers had to set personal performance targets in compacts of Timmer's overall design, and in so doing, either buy in to the new compacts or indirectly signal that they didn't agree.

In the budget reviews which started the day after Timmer's kick-off speech, managers translated their personal targets into budgets that they had to commit explicitly to achieving. For Timmer, these follow-up meetings went beyond simple budget reviews.

'The budget review should reflect a searching, thorough process on the fundamentals of the business. … Philips managers will have to handle … their budget as a personal contract. It will mean keeping your word by following through on your promises.'

To drive home his point, in the days and weeks following the De Ruwenberg meeting, Timmer conducted more one-to-one interviews with senior managers, thus highlighting the significance of individual responsibility for, and contribution to, Operation Centurion. These interviews confirmed the individual commitments to Operation Centurion.

Ask change agents to cascade the change down

The roll out of turnaround change relies on a cascaded wave of co-ordinated projects, each led by a change agent. In many cases, the change agents are existing managers who face the compact choice of becoming a change agent, or getting out of the way.

Once the objectives for Operation Centurion came into focus at the first meetings, the senior managers who bought into the new compacts acted as change agents. They negotiated Centurion compacts with their business unit directors, and that group then took the initiative to the product-group and country management teams. At workshops and training programmes on all levels, change agents led discussions on the objectives and consequences of the change. On each level, the managers discussed their overall goal as a group, and stated what they would be willing to do to achieve the group goal.

Unequivocal message for bystanders

As the Philips story demonstrates, you have to communicate the take-it-or-leave compact framework clearly to employees, sharing information, explaining the need for the change, the new direction, and what it means for people in practice.

To reach bystanders throughout the company, Timmer video taped his kick-off speech on Operation Centurion. He and other senior managers then called 'Town Meetings' where they extolled the virtues of Operation Centurion to thousands – some estimates are as high as one hundred and twenty thousand – via satellite. Shunning decorum and avoiding pronouncements from on high, Timmer communicated in simple, direct phrases that were close to the heart of the ordinary employee. In addition, 'listen to' and progress report sessions took place whenever a member of the General Management Committee visited a business unit. Explicit commitment occurred with the acceptance of new roles after the reorganization.

Rapid reorganization to bring the traditionalists on board

Rapid reorganization burns the bridges to the past, exposes traditionalists to a new reality, and pushes them to redesign their compacts and get on board, or make other arrangements.

At Philips, the reorganization was embedded in the new budgeting and control process. Timmer would no longer tolerate excuses for poor performance. The standard costing system was replaced with a simple one based on actual costs and profits. In the old system, profit estimates were based on standard estimates of what a product would cost; these often had little relation to what it actually cost to make the product. This system had been quick, but ineffective; there were often large discrepancies between estimated and actual profits, and these were explained away by talk of random external factors. From now on, the real financial performance of each business unit was going to be measured by the new actual-cost accounting system. As the new budgeting process got under way, everyone, particularly the traditionalists, began to realize that when it came to the central cost reduction objective of Operation Centurion, there was no place left to hide.

Apart from the systematic appraisal of progress in the budget review meetings between the management board, the product divisions, and the business units, Timmer introduced a wide-ranging training programme of seminars and workshops to provide people with the necessary skills for the new budgeting and control process. He also insisted that promotion and reward be clearly tied to performance all the way to the top of the company. And to reinforce this new performance-based meritocracy, Timmer began hiring top managers from outside, from outside the Netherlands when no internal candidate qualified. Even at the very top, Timmer asked those who didn't keep the promises in their personal contracts with him, including the head of the consumer electronics division, to leave. As a result, by mid-1994, the top management committees, which previously had been dominated by locals, looked quite international. The top six-member board of management included three foreigners, while the 14-member group management committee, including division heads, had only five Dutchmen.

A VIABLE COMPACT FOR THOSE WHO STAY

The key to a viable compact for those who remain after a turnaround is clarity and honesty about their future economic status, based on a clear strategy for future value creation, beyond the lay-offs. At Philips, decisions to hire and fire would no longer be based on political sway or seniority, but rather on strategic objectives and merit. It became clear that patronage and social networking, life-time employment in exchange for loyalty to the company, even at the top, were things of the past. The bystanders and traditionalists knew if they supported the change, as long as they could create strategic value for the company, they had a job. Yet, Timmer could not give his people any guarantee that their compacts would last, except to say that those who performed would move ahead. He left a lot of uncertainty in the air, which kept people on their toes, but made morale fragile.

Ultimately, in the 18 months to the end of 1991, the work force was cut by 22 per cent, or 68,000 people. By making profits a clear priority and quickly flushing resistors out of the system, Timmer improved performance significantly. Between 1990 and 1995, operating profits rose from US$2.2 billion to US$4 billion and the stock price went from 20 guilders to 50.

It is instructive to contrast the Philips experience with that of Porsche, the German sports car maker, where management went further in reducing the risk for those who survived the corporate re-engineering. In the turnaround process, headcount was slashed: one third of the total labour and management was laid off. To those who remained, the 'hard core', the CEO, Wendelin Wiedeking, made a commitment to try to preserve their employment by hiring temporary workers to meet demand (to a limit of 20 per cent hires on the production floor). He made it quite clear to the temporary workers that their contract was temporary; these were the terms under which they were hired. To the permanent workers, this arrangement offered the best chance of holding their jobs. In Wiedeking's view, this new hiring policy not only gave Porsche greater flexibility, but it was also much more honest with the two categories of workers, who now knew exactly where they stood.

PITFALL AFTER TURNAROUND: HUBRIS OF THE COMMANDER

If turnaround is to succeed in the long run, commanders have to avoid the pitfall of excessive hubris. Success in managing crisis often creates boundless self-confidence. Commanders begin to trust their intuition and judgement more and more exclusively, feel more and more infallible in their approach to change, and step out beyond their abilities. When the environment starts shifting, or they start pushing into areas where their expertise is longer applicable, they do not realize how exposed they are. This leads them to keep imposing less and less viable compacts on their people, until the turnaround starts to crumble from within.

At Philips, Timmer's attempts to find a blockbuster new product reflect this classic pitfall which often arises after the turnaround has been accomplished. Timmer repeatedly pushed hard for large new product introductions. They were disasters: DCC, a digital tape cassette system flopped, while interactive CD-ROMs and SRAM memory chips each cost US$1 billion before the plug was pulled. These disasters eventually accumulated into a loss of US$313 million in 1996, and Timmer resigned in favour of Cor Boonstra. After the weak product lines had been cleared out, however, Philips returned in 1997 to record profits.

TASKFORCE COMPACT RENEWAL

MEDOIL: INTENSIVE SOLICITATION OF DIFFERENT VIEWS

'Why mess with it?' asked the senior manager of production and drilling at Medoil, the oil and gas subsidary of a German multinational. He saw no need for a process re-engineering task force; the company was doing well. The men running the offshore production platforms, many of whom had been with the company for more than ten years, were especially cynical: 'This is another one of those things cooked up at headquarters that has got nothing to do with reality. We've seen it all before.'

To deal with this resistance, the managing director, Robert Kohl, decided to face the cynicism of the production men and the manager on their own turf – out on the platforms in the North Sea. He wanted to demonstrate how much money the company could save by re-engineering its processes to integrate across the three existing departments. In preparation, he intensively solicited suggestions throughout the company for the re-engineering task force, so that the latter could make fully informed recommendations, and so that the production men would know he was not just pandering to them when he came to discuss their concerns.

TASKFORCE APPROACH TO COMPACT RENEWAL

To get people to buy into new compacts that support taskforce change, you have to make the role of the task forces absolutely clear. You have to ensure that the task forces solicit the opinions of all the relevant players, especially the bystanders, and give everyone the chance to commit fully once the taskforce recommendations are accepted. The key ingredients in this approach to compact renewal are outlined below:

Taskforce approach to compact renewal

Style:	Chairman, intensive solicitation of opinions.
Design:	Top down.
Renewal sequence and tactics:	1. Ask change agents to staff task forces.
	2. Ensure that task forces solicit bystanders' opinions.
	3. Confront resistors with a choice of buying in or out.
	4. Put traditionalists into implementation groups.
Key success factor:	Give everyone the chance to commit, once the task forces have finished.
Pitfall:	Too many task forces confuse the change effort.

On his promotion, Robert Kohl knew that the company was suffering from errors, safety problems, and cost overruns in its pipeline and North Sea platform operations. He was determined to do something. Yet, the company was still performing well, so the change pressure was weak. Also, the development, construction, and production departments operated as separate silos, co-operation was non-existent, and the resistance to the change was high. Within this classic setting of weak change pressure and strong resistance, Kohl set up a task force nominated by the three departmental managers, plus a member from the safety team. The mandate of the task force was to describe, and then redesign, the primary corporate processes that cut across the three departments.

CHAIRMAN-STYLE LEADERSHIP COMPACT

Robert Kohl was a classic chairman, with a strong preference for chairing and co-ordinating work groups, synthesizing different points of view with planning, budgets and action plans, policies and procedures.

With his superiors on the board, Kohl set up a personal compact based on a mandate to improve divisional performance. With his subordinates, he preferred to set up compacts in which he played more of a sponsoring and controlling role, rather than managing the change effort directly himself. He asked a senior manager with experience in change management to help him lead the change effort. This gave him the flexibility to act as the overall co-ordinator of the change, rather than as the re-engineering taskforce leader.

The unco-operative response of the people on the production platforms was reinforced by their lack of contact with the rest of the organization; they were either on the platforms, or on leave, but almost never at head office. As a result, they responded in three ways:

- as bystanders who had the broader skills to adapt to the new cross-departmental processes but were not convinced things would really change
- as traditionalists who didn't have the skills
- as resistors like the production managers who would lose power.

The managing director began to see that if the task force was going to have any chance of collecting the detailed information on current processes that it needed to do its job, he had a big selling job on his hands.

TYPICAL TASKFORCE COMPACT

Those asked to join off-line task forces automatically become a class apart. They need clarity to reduce the uncertainty about the potential implications of what they are doing. They need the support of all relevant players to ensure that they get the information and organizational space to do the job. If the task forces are to perform, their members must have the confidence that they will get the necessary support and be assessed on the merit of their contribution, rather than position, with sufficient recognition and other intangibles to make participation worthwhile. Some of the features that should included in the economic dimension of taskforce compacts are indicated below:

Economic dimension of taskforce compacts

What am I supposed to do?	Participate in team to develop change agenda
What help will I get?	Resources and full support from relevant players
How will I be measured?	Merit, plus team performance
What rewards will I get?	Recognition, enhanced promotion potential, etc.

SEQUENCE AND TACTICS FOR COMPACT RENEWAL DURING TASKFORCE CHANGE

The first step in orchestrating taskforce change is to seek out change agents to lead the task forces. These may be hard to find, because the uncertainty in the change direction causes many people to respond as bystanders and, especially, as traditionalists in a closed organization like Medoil. The change agents in this case were mainly younger managers and supervisors.

Ask the change agents to flesh out the direction of the change

At Medoil, the process re-engineering team had a clear compact: analyze and diagnose the existing processes for redundancy and inefficiency, and redesign them, taking account of the simplification that IT can support. Expert advice was provided on how to carry out business process re-engineering. The output of the projects could be precisely measured in terms of time and costs saved, as well as increased employee safety. In terms of rewards, the high visibility of the teams meant that the members' careers would be strongly affected by the outcome of the projects.

The social dimension of these compacts involved a shared willingness to question every working assumption, to pursue improvement with almost radical fervour, and to play by the implicit rules of the team. The psychological attraction of these compacts was the challenge to redesign processes and systems that affected everyone and hadn't been put under a lens since they'd first been put in place. A further attraction was the high stakes involved: if the projects were successful, the impact would be felt throughout the organization and show up on the bottom-line; if they failed in having much impact, the hoop-la surrounding them meant that people would not quickly forget.

Intense solicitation of opinion to bring bystanders on board

Selling the change initiative to bystanders during taskforce change requires intense solicitation of their opinion. Prior to Robert Kohl's appointment, relations at Medoil had been characterized by a direct, somewhat confrontational and formal style, reflecting a relatively high power distance, as was customary in German companies. Although he realized that he could not change this overnight, Kohl believed that, for the task force and the process re-engineering to succeed, he was going to have to set a new tone at Medoil. To implement the recommendations of the task force and co-ordinate the activities of the steering committee and various implementation teams, informal consultation, not confrontation, was a must. With this in mind, Kohl started a series of interdepartmental discussions while the task force was doing its work. These discussions began to break down the fences between the departments and provide original views on the design of the new organizational processes.

After the opening set of meetings for senior and middle managers at headquarters, Kohl began a tour of the platforms. During each visit, he explained how value was created in the business, he outlined the problem of errors and losses, and he underscored the need for cost control. Most importantly, however, he opened up a frank, face-to-face dialogue about the men's frustrations with earlier change efforts and the importance of sharing their views to make this one work.

Robert Kohl's willingness to meet his people as equals out in the field made a deep impression on them. He was spearheading the way to a new, consultative (as opposed to a power-based) set of values and informal rules that encouraged commitment to the change effort. This commitment would be based on a new openness to the opinions of others. By laying himself open on sensitive issues with hardened and cynical employees, Kohl demonstrated his commitment to what he was advocating. As a result, more and more people were willing, albeit grudgingly, to give him the benefit of the doubt and consider taking the risk of co-operating and sharing their views.

Confront the resistors to prevent them from undermining the taskforces

During taskforce change, when the pressure is often too weak to give leaders the legitimacy of turnaround change to force out resistors, you have to be more circumspect. You need to take a multi-pronged approach to crowd the resistors out with increased pressure. You need enough time to identify the value-creating idea and develop support for it, so that the resistors can feel their influence waning and see that their cause is lost.

At Medoil, several production managers openly resisted the idea that their processes could be improved through integration. Kohl decided to enlist the aid of the change agents indirectly to pressure the resistors. He organized a senior management workshop to discuss the output of the task force, so the resistors would be exposed to the enthusiasm of the change agents and the advantages of the new processes. Groups worked out how the new processes would be cascaded down. The resistors saw there was no turning back when Kohl confronted them with his expectations: commit to the implementation process by accepting explicit assignments. As Kohl put it, 'I want us to leave the past. I want you to join me in shaping the future, by helping to lead the implementation process. ... For those who have difficulty with this, we can make alternative arrangements'. Several production managers left.

Once the senior resistors were gone, Kohl was ready to lock in the commitment of the bystanders, mainly the business unit managers, and through them, the department heads. He achieved this with 'Zielvereinbarung' (goal setting). The goal setting was done in process teams, with each individual making a commitment to provide resources, or fill a role in the new process.

In contrast to what happens during turnaround, the process was consultative and iterative, requiring people to attend several meetings, because each individual commitment depended on what his business unit, or department, was willing to commit: after the process group meeting, each manager went to his unit to see what they could commit, and then back to his process group to lock in the commitment. The goal-setting process was linked to the budgeting process and to a new performance appraisal system, including a fixed component associated with the normal job, and a variable component based on performance relative to personal and change-project goals.

Implementation groups for the traditionalists

To sway the mass of traditionalists that typically accompanies taskforce change, you have to allay their insecurity. Having the change agents flesh out the details of the change, neutralizing the resistors, and converting the bystanders to the implementation effort, lays the groundwork. However, you also have to find appropriate roles in the implementation groups and provide training to give the traditionalists the working security they need to turn the taskforce recommendations into practice.

The new process groups needed specialist skills that, in many cases, only certain traditionalists could provide. Designing attractive new compacts for these people was relatively easy. The problems came with traditionalist employees out on the platforms who had to join teams of unfamiliar people, for example, the exploration project process group that included numerous headquarters staff. At first, there was disbelief that they would have to work with the 'staff eggheads', but then they discovered they had met many of their future process colleagues during the managing director's interdepartmental discussion groups. As a result, when the process skills training got underway, the groups began to function remarkably well. Within a year, the initial cost reduction, cycle time, and safety targets had been met, or exceeded.

GIVE EVERYONE THE OPPORTUNITY TO COMMIT

In other cases of taskforce change, special groups have been formed to accommodate traditionalists. For example, special support groups staffed by traditionalists were formed to re-engineer the gold mining process at the Harmony Gold Mine in South Africa. Prior to the change, 11 hierarchical levels separated the lowest miner underground from the mine manager on the surface. All jobs were specialized, with some, like blasting out the rock face, reserved for white miners with special certificates of qualification. As the price of gold dropped, the quality of the ore mined deteriorated, and the wages of black miners increased, cost reduction became imperative. But the rigidity of the existing structure and the related personal compacts blocked real change. People with protected positions were unwilling to sacrifice their privileges. Only when a new manager took over with the mandate to cut costs or close the mine did people begin to accept the need for change. He invited the key players to join him in a task force to redesign the business system from top to bottom.

The redesigned system was centred around multi-skilled teams at the ore face with a stake in operating profit responsibility (based on ore extracted minus controllable costs). But many of the protected operators refused to risk linking their salaries to profits. As classic traditionalists, they wanted something more secure. The design team proposed that, for each section of the mine, a support group be formed to service the front-line teams with mining materials, ore transport, and other logistics. The support groups would be cost centres, with fixed salaries and bonuses linked to cost targets. Many of the traditionalists found this compact much more appealing. Each support group with its related front-line groups formed a relatively independent, lean production system. The support groups were not only crucial to the new production system, they also encouraged many of the traditional mining types to renew their personal compacts to support the change.

PITFALL DURING TASKFORCE CHANGE: TOO MANY CONFLICTING PROJECTS

One of the big risks of taskforce change is too many task forces with conflicting objectives. Setting them up is easy for the chairman-style leader, who is usually good at co-ordinating groups and getting the necessary approval of the stakeholders. But the emphasis on taskforce process makes the leader susceptible to quick fixes. As a result, whenever a new change force emerges, there may be a tendency to set up yet another task force, armed with the latest external management fad. Companies run like this are often overburdened with new change initiatives, many of which never get beyond the formal roll out: total quality management, followed by downsizing, process re-engineering, adding customer value for growth, and so on. Under these conditions, however, meaningful compact renewal on the front line is impossible. Compact renewal only works when it is focused.

WIDESPREAD
PARTICIPATIVE
COMPACT RENEWAL

FORD OF EUROPE: A NEED FOR WIDESPREAD COLLABORATION

'The next phase will not be easy to identify and will call for much creative thinking and acceptance of major conceptual change as well as determination in implementation. The improvements necessary to achieve the targets cannot be made only by individual organization components, nor can they be made in the traditional "task and achieve" way. I believe a more participative approach offers the best chance of success.'

To break through to the next level of efficiency, Murray Reichenstein, vice-president of finance at Ford of Europe (FOE), believed that the firm needed a different type of effort from what had been done before. Previously, a three-year downsizing effort designed to catch up with the Japanese had been only partially successful. Most of the drop in headcount was achieved in the first year; in some departments only two thirds of the planned cost reduction was achieved over the three years. Instead of the traditional Ford practice of task forces, the top management team was convinced that a much more widely participative and collaborative effort was now called for.

When FOE realized that its whole culture was still hopelessly top heavy and over controlled relative to its Japanese competitors, management knew that working habits would have to change fundamentally. The only way of significantly cutting costs further was to develop a new way of working together, at the top, pushing decision-making down to the front line, and training the employees to take responsibility for quality and control. Although Ford had never done anything like this before, the executive committee decided it had no choice.

Exactly how this was to be done was unclear. So, top-down turnaround was impossible. On the other hand, task forces could not possibly generate the 'major conceptual change and determination in implementation'. Yet, the previous round of change had opened up the organization. People knew that the targets had not been met, they were sensitive to the need for further change, and many expected to be involved. Ford of Europe was potentially ready for widespread participative change.

WIDESPREAD PARTICIPATIVE APPROACH TO COMPACT RENEWAL

To get compact renewal in a widespread participative mode, you have first to develop a widely shared awareness of the need for change, followed by a shared understanding of what has to be done, and most important, a widely shared commitment to action. The key elements in this process of compact renewal are listed below:

Widespread participative approach to compact renewal

Style:	Coach, collaborative.
Design:	Top-down, bottom-up.
Renewal sequence and tactics:	1. Ask change agents to facilitate participation.
	2. Initiate widespread collaboration with bystanders on change need and direction.
	3. Crowd out resistors with growing support.
	4. Involve traditionalists in network of linked teams.
Key success factor:	Widespread shared commitment to action.
Pitfall:	Process drives out value creation.

COACHING STYLE LEADERSHIP COMPACT

The change agents at FOE were the more aggressive managers in the national sales organizations and some of the production managers. They were chafing under the tight central control of the finance department, which dictated pricing and overall production planning decisions. Most of the sales and production managers, however, were not sure they wanted the extra risk of more decision-making responsibility and thus responded as bystanders to the comments of

Reichenstein and other members of the executive committee. Some of the older managers, who lacked the expertise to take on more responsibility, could be classified as traditionalists. The central financial and business planning staff were likely to resist their 'emasculation' and could exploit the inconsistencies and inevitable mistakes that would be made by the front-line managers early on.

None of the senior executives at FOE felt comfortable leading the actual process of participative change. They called a member of a Kansas City firm of behavioural consultants to their headquarters in Brentwood, Essex, to help the executive committee with the process on a daily basis.

This consultant had the classic profile of a coach who could take advantage of the organizational openness to involve most of the people in working out the direction of the change and implementing it. With her clients, the top management, she set up a change leadership compact based on an open informal mandate that gave her the organizational flexibility to form and nurture teams. With the subordinates, she approached compact renewal in a broadly inclusive manner, working incrementally to bring people on board to deal with the change.

Pushing decision making down to the front line meant increasing people's responsibility and scope for problem solving and practice sharing. To help them cope with the extra risk, senior management got involved in coaching on all levels to help forge the linkage between the new decision making, cost reduction objectives, and the individual compacts. As a result, the design of the compact details was very much of a joint effort. Moreover, new processes for practice exchange created horizontal coaching between the individuals in different departments, which further integrated the effort.

SEQUENCE AND TACTICS FOR WIDESPREAD PARTICIPATIVE COMPACT RENEWAL

You have to start with the change agents, asking them to run the widespread dialogue that provides the context for the numerous bystanders. With support from the change agents and converted bystanders, you can create a shared awareness about the need for change and develop a common understanding about the right change direction. Once the detailed impact of the change becomes apparent, however, it is likely to bring the resistors out into the open. Before putting the full change organization and necessary support in place, you have to deal with the resistors, in order to get a widespread commitment to action from the traditionalists.

Ask the change agents to facilitate participation

The challenge for change agents in participative change is not so much on the economic dimension, because a wide set of people, including the bystanders, will be involved in working out the value-creating ideas, but rather on the social dimension, or more specifically, on designing and facilitating the participative process itself. What is involved here is not merely the change process, but the ongoing process of decentralized decision making.

For change to succeed at Ford of Europe, the change agents had to take charge of the new process. Ford set up a multi-functional steering committee of the best senior people who had been agitating for decentralization. They in turn identified a network of change agents to lead and integrate the dialogue on how the new decision-making process would work. The steering committee also asked another set of change agents to set up training and project work throughout the organization, to give front-line managers the tools and confidence needed to take more decisions, and the employees what they needed for continual improvement.

Widespread collaboration with bystanders to flesh out value-creating ideas

The bystanders are key to the success of participative change. In the relatively open organizations typical of the right context for participative change, if you tell bystanders what to do (as in top-down turnaround), or ask them merely to provide information to task forces, they will suspect you don't trust them. To get them involved, you have to ask them to help flesh out the change direction. Dialogue between change leaders, change agents, team members and peers is the natural way of developing a shared awareness and common understanding with the bystanders about what has to be done. Once bystanders have helped to work out the value-creating idea, you can ask them to signal their commitment by agreeing to help lead the implementation.

At FOE, management gave special attention to getting the upper and middle manager bystanders from different functions into lateral dialogue on the implications of the cultural change. To give front-line people the confidence needed to take on more decisions, Ford's management signalled their willingness to open up. Interpersonal relations at Ford, heavily influenced by hierarchy, were intolerant of failure and confrontational in tone. The new change effort had to 'operate with a minimum of formality to help eliminate organizational conflict – a non-partisan attitude (was) essential'.

In a series of meetings, the top managers from all over Europe met to initiate work on a more open approach to the points of conflict between them and, thereby, gradually to replace confrontational styles with more co-operative ones. The second of these meetings, at the Montreux Palace Hotel, Switzerland, for example, provided anonymous feedback on the most irritating practices of each of the functional groups, as seen by members of the other functions. Thus, finance was criticized among other things for 'over-control', 'too much criticism after the event', and for 'too much influence in decision making'. Feedback of this kind helped all the groups see how their behaviour would have to change to create a leaner company. The central staff, in particular, would have to shift from a decision-making and controlling role to more of a supporting one.

As Ford's senior management signalled the outlines of the new social compact they had in mind, they were aware that the change process, being participative, would not be fully under their control. The whole internal culture would change, and their own decision-making styles would have to evolve. There were intensive discussions with sales and production managers from all the countries about which decisions the front liners should take, which they should have veto power over, and which they should be consulted on. These discussions were messy at first.

Some of the participants, in typical bystander fashion, argued that the change would only create unnecessary confusion; the status quo was much better. It was only after grappling with the bench-marking studies of the Japanese competitors and the central issue of cost reduction, that they finally came to grips with the need for real change. The eventual recommendations on decision making from these groups varied mainly between the large and smaller countries, but were remarkably similar in their approach to the reinforcement of continual improvement and the internal sharing of best practice. This round of discussions ended with the participants agreeing individually to lead or participate in teams as part of the implementation process.

Crowd out resistors with growing support

Once the direction of the participative effort becomes clear with the commitment of the bystanders, resistors will move to counter the explicit threat to their position. Rather than a frontal attack, which would be too obviously self-serving, they often take the high ground by arguing that all the effort being put into the participative process isn't creating any value. And they will not be entirely wrong, because up to this point the change effort will not have produced many results. This argument is particularly appealing to threatened traditionalists. At this critical moment, when the change effort may be discredited, you have to hold your ground. Confront the resistors with the choice: buy in, or out.

Towards the end of the discussions on the design of the new decision-making processes and work approach at FOE, resistors attacked the complexity and uncertainty in the whole scheme. The executive committee intervened to say that there was no going back. Either these people were willing to lead one of the implementation teams, or not. Some resignations and reassignments followed.

Network of linked teams for shared commitment to action from traditionalists

Typically, you can gain a shared commitment to action by forming a network of linked teams led by the change agents and converted bystanders. You link each team vertically to its internal or external customers and suppliers, and horizontally, by encouraging the sharing of best practice. Traditionalists will appreciate your support for personal adaptation and development, a common part of the compacts of these teams.

To support the traditionalists who lacked the necessary skills, FOE initiated large-scale training programmes to facilitate employee and worker involvement in continual improvement that was linked directly to the overall cost reduction targets. In addition, the steering committee put an interlocking set of multi-functional teams in place to implement the recommendations on best practice sharing for increased efficiency and work streamlining. Team leaders could decide on the membership of these teams, but overall, top management recommended a broad range of participation. As the set of teams expanded, most people in the organization got involved.

However, decentralized decision making and on-line continual improvement threatened the security of the traditionalists. To reduce the perceived risk, management made a commitment to avoid involuntary dismissals:

'It is important that all our people understand the need for efficiency improvement and want to participate; it is therefore essential that they also understand that the primary objective is to eliminate non-essential work and that any saving in human resource will be made through attrition and voluntary programmes of termination. In the event this is not immediately achievable, those personnel whose jobs may be eliminated or reduced will be used to support the effort towards further streamlining practices.'

Since the senior management group had stuck to its commitments on this score during the first round of change, it still had credibility.

As the new decision-making processes began to take root, FOE started to benefit not only from the cost savings, but also from the greater flexibility on the front line, all of which contributed to the dramatic improvements on the bottom line. In the late eighties, FOE was very successful. However, as often happens, management did not take the next step to ongoing change, so the performance could not be sustained. As a result, in the late nineties, FOE was again a candidate for major change.

IMPORTANCE OF A WIDESPREAD COMMITMENT TO ACTION

To make widespread participation effective, you have to get widespread commitment to action. To move your people to action, you must get beyond discussing the need for change and understanding what is wrong. FOE did this by putting people into the multifunctional teams with an explicit compact to implement the recommendations developed during the earlier rounds of discussion.

Without an explicit, widespread opportunity to participate in implementation, the participative process gradually grinds to a halt. The case of a Hong Kong bank illustrates this nicely.

After lots of discussion on several levels at the bank, employee groups met once a week from 6pm to 8pm to begin fixing quality norms. But the groups could not reach a consensus and began to lose confidence; not only were they making no progress, they started getting negative feedback from resistors who could not see any results. One of the team members confessed that he didn't find the process 'real', but rather found it 'a nice intellectual exercise'. The breakthrough only occurred when the manager and department heads defined the quality norms and asked for concrete suggestions on how customer service could be improved to meet them. This gave everyone a simple, unambiguous way of participating in the change created a widespread commitment to action, and left the resistors with the choice of complying, or being exposed.

The experience at other companies suggests that you can put together a highly elaborate network of linked teams explicitly to integrate many people into a common commitment to action. The indispensable element for each team is a clear action mandate and linkage to the other teams.

The elaborate nature of the team network that designed Boeing Aircraft's new 777 passenger jet is especially striking. The first layer of teams was made up of more than 200 cross-functional teams of 5 to 15 people from different departments, with each team being responsible for the design of a different part of the plane, like the tail, the flaps, and so on. The second layer comprised 25 to 30 two-person teams, with a member each from engineering and operations, responsible for facilitating and monitoring the progress of the design teams. These second tier teams were responsible for solving problems faced by the design teams and taking large issues to the top for resolution. At the top was a management team of senior managers from each of the functional disciplines. The team bore the full responsibility for ensuring that a particular plane be built according to the overall objectives and on time. Yet, the vertical lines of communication were not sufficient to co-ordinate the whole project. Design problems occured because the wing teams, for example, didn't know exactly how the cockpit teams were putting their part of the plane together. So the project management added a fourth type of team, which they called 'airplane integration teams'. These five teams, with 12 to 15 members drawn from the design teams, had access to every person and every piece of information on the project.

PITFALL IN WIDESPREAD PARTICIPATION: PROCESS DRIVES OUT VALUE CREATION

One of the big risks in participative change is the cultural process getting in the way of economic value creation. You can become so focused on trying to develop a participative culture that you lose sight of its ultimate purpose, which is to create value, as the experience of Jan Carlson's tenure at Scandinavian Airlines demonstrates.

When Carlson took over as president, SAS invested heavily in the Carlson team-inspired mission of becoming the Businessman's Airline. The centrepiece of the programme was a new concept of service based on a cultural revolution at SAS that put front-line employees into participative teams, and gave the teams freedom to take responsibility for their ideas, decisions, and actions. Putting these compacts in place involved extensive coaching and training throughout the company. As a next step, Carlson and his team came up with the concept of door-to-door service and one-stop business travel shopping. When the downturn hit in the early 1990s, however, SAS's costs were hopelessly out of line. Instead of ordering cost reduction from the top down, or stepping back and giving the cost cutters a compact to turn the company around financially, Carlson involved the company in a process of complex alliance discussions with Swissair and KLM. The collapse of these negotiations marked the end of SAS's growth strategy – and Carlson's downfall. Carlson's participative approach obscured the need for cost reduction and was completely overtaken by events.

COMPACT RENEWAL FOR BOTTOM-UP INITIATIVES

PERFORMANCE CHEMICALS: PROVOCATIVE STIMULUS FOR BOTTOM-UP INITIATIVES

'We seize an opportunity the moment it presents itself, and we work the details day-in and day-out to maintain our competitive edge. We focus on high technology markets where our superior assets provide the marketing advantage, and in geographical areas where our capabilities assure the very best customer service.'

With these words, John Norman, the manager of the Performance Chemicals division of a major multinational, opened a cross-functional workshop on the sharing of best innovation and business development practice.

Customers were clamouring for more service and custom-made products, thereby creating a clear direction for change. A previous downsizing had opened the organization up, increasing competence, making people more ready for change. In brief, the context was right for bottom-up initiatives. With this in mind, Norman had asked the sales force to take the initiative, and put incentives in place. But the people in the field continued calling on the over-worked technology people from the central laboratory to solve their technical problems.

So, he took the controversial step of banning travel by central laboratory scientists into the field. Both the sales and the lab people cried foul: how could they possibly respond to customer needs? In response, John Norman encouraged the change agents to capitalize on their new freedom to innovate without interference from the lab, and invited them to the cross-functional workshop for a first review of how things were going.

BOTTOM-UP INITIATIVES APPROACH TO COMPACT RENEWAL

To get bottom-up initiatives, you have to stimulate and inspire people

129

to design entrepreneurial compacts for themselves, by challenging the change agents to begin taking initiative, and encouraging bystanders to imitate them. A key ingredient is a new social compact that gives people the freedom to experiment.

Bottom-up initiatives approach to compact renewal

Style:	Inspirational, provocative.
Design:	Bottom-up.
Renewal sequence and tactics:	1. Challenge change agents to take business initiative.
	2. Encourage bystanders to imitate.
	3. Integrate traditionalists into the entrepreneurial teams.
	4. Throw down performance challenge to resistors.
Key success factor:	A new social compact that supports initiative.
Pitfall:	*Laissez-faire* results in confusion.

INSPIRATIONAL STYLE LEADERSHIP COMPACT

With his superiors, Norman had a compact based on an informal, open-ended mandate and individual discretion on how to improve the performance of the subsidiary. With his subordinates, the sales engineers, he wanted a compact that would challenge them to go beyond their experience, with the necessary training, resources, scope, and support for risk taking. This meant not only giving people enough organizational scope and resources, but also ensuring that customers were providing sufficiently strong signals, enough information about their problems, to guide the bottom-up design.

The withdrawal of scientific support from the field, together with the customer demands, split the sales engineers into three camps:

- change agents who saw the new situation as an opportunity to show what they could do without the interference of the technical people
- bystanders with customers who were not demanding
- resistors, feeling they didn't have the skills, who started complaining they would lose key customers.

The central laboratories also split into three camps:

- bystanders, comprising most of the staff who didn't believe the new policy would work
- traditionalists who had never really been involved in the field and wanted to keep it that way
- the laboratory managers who, wanting to keep their influence in the field, resisted the move as not being in the customers' interests.

John Norman sensed that potential change agents out in the field wanted to break loose from the interference of the lab and what they needed was a trigger to do so. He also realized there was a morale problem among the people in the laboratory, who saw themselves not only as stretched in manpower, but also as 'slaves' to the sales force. In brief, the market was clamouring for more customized products, which the technology group was unable to deliver. Norman decided he had to have more innovation out in the field and the only way he was going to get it, was to inspire and provoke the sales engineers into action.

COMPACT RENEWAL SEQUENCE AND TACTICS FOR BOTTOM-UP INITIATIVES

Bottom-up initiatives are built on empowerment (an overworked word which makes sense in this context). You have to empower change agents to drive the change effort spontaneously, by taking initiative. The success stories of the change agents then draw in the bystanders, reinforcing the new rules of the game, thereby reducing the apparent risk of taking initiative. The number of change agents and converted bystanders, plus the strength of the change force, makes it difficult for resistors to build a case for opposing the change. As the change effort gathers momentum, the traditionalists begin to feel safe about joining in and this snowball effect puts resistors onto the defensive.

Challenge change agents to propose new initiatives

At Performance Chemicals, the removal of the lab people from the field was the trigger that provided the scope for bottom-up compact renewal in the field. The sales people were forced to start custom-mixing chemicals on site themselves with advice from the lab over the phone. After some initial trial and error, this started to produce much quicker response to customer requests. In addition, the sales people began to tackle new problems and started coming up with new products. The customers were impressed, the sales people gained confidence, and business began to pick up rapidly. The new economic compacts the change agents designed for themselves included the following:

New economic compact for sales engineers at performance chemicals

What am I supposed to do?	Customize products and look for new product ideas
What help will I get?	Information from customers, advice from lab over the phone
How will I be measured?	Sales targets, business development and innovation
What's in it for me?	Secure my job, commissions from growth

Bottom-up initiatives depend on easy access to people and ideas, that is, direct, informal relationships based on a low power distance, and a willingness to confront reality. At Performance Chemicals, Norman encouraged this by removing the barriers between the functional groups, providing support for cross-functional co-operation to solve customer problems, and shared rewards for virtual teams of sales engineers, lab people, and others, including customer representatives. The reward system was geared to those who not only delivered results, but also supported others in their innovation efforts. Most importantly, Norman organized monthly reviews with each sales engineer to assess progress on new initiatives. These personal reviews provided the process for ironing out the details of the individual compacts and ensuring alignment with the divisional objectives.

Encourage bystanders to imitate the change agents

Once the change agents start scoring successes, simple processes can be put in place so the bystanders see and hear what the change is all about. The change leadership can reinforce this bandwagon effect by giving individual feedback to those bystanders who convert to change agent activity, and by demonstrating the acceptability of trial and error.

At Performance Chemicals, John Norman kept repeating his message at every available opportunity: 'Innovation to create value for our customers is the key to the future … Some failures are inevitable, but that's the way we are going to learn.' The cross-functional workshops on best innovation practice provided an open forum for frank discussion of individual sales force innovation, and how best to go about it. Recognition went to those who had taken successful initiatives, but failures were also used as case studies. This was a delicate process: trying to understand what went wrong, while giving credit for taking initiative. Proposals also emerged from the workshops that called for change at the headquarters. The managers concerned had to respond to proposals on the spot, or at the latest within a few weeks.

The innovation practice sharing workshops gave bystanders the opportunity to hear what the change agents were doing. The bystanders realized what could be done for apparently non-demanding customers to grow their business. Meanwhile the individual monthly reviews gave Norman the chance to coax them on board and push for a more innovative sales approach. When they started offering more customized products and services on a trial basis, their less demanding customers started to see the latent potential for cost reduction, and shorter exploration and drilling times in their own business. This in turn not only generated new demand, but made these customers more and more dependent on Performance Chemicals for their own improved results.

The bystanders in the central labs were soon also under pressure to co-operate. The success stories presented at the innovation workshops demonstrated that the sales engineers were quite capable of innovating. Norman used personal recognition and bonuses for those who had provided input to successful field innovation, to encourage compact renewal by the lab bystanders. As the word got around the labs, the lab people became much more co-operative when the sales engineers called in for advice. The researchers began to volunteer their assistance and tie their search for new compounds to substances which could be more easily adapted in the field.

Integrate traditionalists into the self-managing teams

The initiatives started by change agents and bystanders typically lead to self-managed teams. The psychological benefit of the compacts of self-managed team members in large part reflects the satisfaction of intense teamwork. For traditionalists, with their affinity for the psychological support available in a good team, the emotional component in self-managed teams is a strong motivator. The relative autonomy of the teams causes the members to be heavily dependent on one another, with a lot of learning and training going on informally within the team. When a team performs and begins to achieve the goals it has set itself, the result is a very strong, often highly emotional commitment that traditionalists especially cannot resist.

As the new innovation effort in the labs of Performance Chemicals began to pick up steam, Norman announced that the time had come for everyone to be part of the new aggressive sales approach. Everyone, including the central laboratory traditionalists who had rarely been out in the field before the change, was to be part of the monthly innovation review process. They were invited to join one of the new virtual teams forming between the labs and the sales engineers, or one of the lab research projects where their know-how was deemed to be critical. Their participation in these teams soon turned them into supporters of intensive lab-field co-operation, especially when some of their projects got recognition at the innovation practice workshops.

Throw down a performance challenge to deal with resistors

Resistance to bottom-up initiatives often comes from those who do not want to buy in to the supporting values and behaviour, people who are afraid to take the risk themselves, or are threatened by the progress of others. Discussions during the monthly review at Performance Chemicals, with resistors in the field who had yet to show signs of innovative effort, revealed a lack of the necessary technical skills.

Norman decided to challenge the recalcitrant sales engineers to match the performance of the change agents. It was nine months since the lab travel ban. Norman declared that it was time for section leaders from the labs to update themselves on the new developments and customer needs in the field. He asked the section leaders to put together a flexible training programme for the sales engineers based on new developments in the lab and their observations during the field trip. To demonstrate their commitment, the sales engineers had to put together a personal development plan, incorporating pieces of the lab training programme, with the option of taking selected courses at the local technical university near the lab. Progress towards personal development and field innovation objectives were included in the monthly review. About two-thirds of the resistors took the opportunity; the others gradually left.

Dealing with the resistors among the lab managers involved a more top-down approach. (As we shall see in the next chapter, change commonly involves a combination of the basic processes discussed in the last four chapters.) Norman had to sort out the position of the lab managers before trying to bring the bystanders and traditionalists in the labs on board. He did this after the first innovation workshop, when the counterproductive criticism of the lab managers highlighted the need for a new form of co-operation with the labs.

During one of their weekly management meetings, Norman confronted the lab managers with their negative attitude. When they protested their innocence, he went around the table challenging each of them to declare what they were willing to do to support the emerging innovation effort in the field. Although his confidence in their commitments was mixed, Norman had created the opening he needed for the sales engineers to contact the labs for technical advice. Once co-operation gathered momentum on the back of field successes, the lab managers had little choice but to confirm that they were behind the effort.

The results over the last year were impressive in terms of the new products and contracts achieved. These included the on-site development of a new demulsifier for the Saudi market, a new water soluble corrosion inhibitor that solved a persistent down-hole corrosion problem, a breakthrough in the West African market that led to a large increase in market share, and so on. Many of these developments involved intensive cross-functional co-operation and team work. As Norman put it in his closing remarks at the innovation workshop:

> 'Although my question (on innovative practice) was addressed to you as individuals, many of the replies used the words "multifunctional team". This really tells us about the progress our organization has made.'

THE SOCIAL COMPACT IS CENTRAL TO BOTTOM-UP INITIATIVES

With the strong external change forces providing the direction of the change, the key to success of bottom-up initiatives is the new social compact (see Chapter 14). Beyond information sharing and involvement, bottom-up initiatives require, as the Performance Chemicals example illustrates, a shared set of values and informal rules about the role of experimentation and entrepreneurship in the company. Yet, developing new business is a high risk activity with a low success rate. To get change agents and others to accept the challenge, you have to nurture a social compact with acceptance of failure built into the informal rules of the game. A shared appreciation of initiative, merit, and money as well as intangibles, is essential to provide the right climate for experimentation and support for entrepreneurship. In addition, you have to stimulate intensive communication across boundaries, especially with customers, and provide easy access to the necessary resources.

PITFALL IN BOTTOM-UP INITIATIVES: CONFUSION FROM TOO MUCH *LAISSEZ-FAIRE*

Successfully stimulating bottom-up initiatives is very much a matter of context. When the context is wrong, say, in the middle of a crisis, or when process re-engineering is called for, bottom-up initiatives can be the main obstacle to change. Having everybody running around pursuing their own growth opportunities, can be a recipe for disaster.

The financial services industry is full of hands-off, inspirational leaders presiding with arms-length compacts over what can be very high risk activities. Being hands-off, these leaders have a tendency to offer their people new compacts for bottom-up initiatives, even when the direction of the change is unclear. As a result, the front-liners in financial services often walk in droves over the same financial cliff. Thus, the 1970s real estate lending crisis was followed by the crisis in third world debt, which was followed by the 1980s crisis in junk bonds, and the 1990s crises, first in real estate, and then in emerging markets and Asian debt. These crises were precipitated by too much *laissez-faire*, not enough control of frontliners pursuing market opportunities of declining quality. Whereas bottom-up initiatives often are the best way of capturing share in new and strongly growing markets, they can be a disaster when that growth dries up.

DEALING WITH THE POLITICS OF COMPACT RENEWAL

DELTA AUTO: THE POLITICS OF COMPACT RENEWAL

'Forget about all this stuff from headquarters. It's just a bunch of arrogant young idiots trying to throw their weight around.' Delta Auto, the major automobile manufacturer, had just announced that it wanted to form new relationships with all its dealers, and this was the response when one of those dealers asked a member of Continental's marketing staff about the new relationship. To stem a loss in market share, Continental wanted to improve dealer relations. This included setting up a more efficient delivery system of consistently high quality products, and a new dealer reward system that required the dealers to co-operate in meeting the manufacturer's standards.

To do this, Continental took a taskforce approach to compact renewal. A group of young managers at head office got the mandate to set up working groups with successful dealers to work out the conditions of the new relationship. The early success of the working groups at developing a smoother, more responsive system soon swayed most of the bystanders among the country managers and senior managers at head office to support the changes.

But this success alarmed the sales and marketing staff, who saw themselves being bypassed. They stirred up objections among the less successful dealers, encouraging them to join the ranks of resistors and oppose the change. Tension increased between the sales and marketing resistors and the young change agents. The attitude of the senior management bystanders became critical: they had the organizational power to withdraw support from, and kill, the change effort, or show their commitment and help make it work. They had to deal with the politics of compact renewal.

HOW TO DEAL WITH THE POLITICS OF COMPACT RENEWAL

Whatever the change process, to orchestrate compact renewal you have to align all the important players with the change effort. This means preventing the resistors from blocking alignment by inciting the traditionalists and bystanders to oppose the change.

How to deal with the politics

A. Develop influence

    – Ensure support of superiors with robust leadership compact.

    – Build change momentum when and wherever possible.

B. Monitor balance of power

    – Monitor milestones.

    – Observe whether compact renewal sequence leads to commitment.

C. Time your intervention

    – At the beginning of the change process.

    – If the balance of power tilts.

    – When a major resource commitment is needed.

DEVELOPING INFLUENCE TO ORCHESTRATE COMPACT RENEWAL

The appropriate way of developing influence depends on how much time you have. The shorter the time available and the more pressing the change, the more you need organizational power to confront the resistors. The amount of power you have acquired over time, especially through the negotiation of your leadership compact, becomes critical. If your superiors are unwilling to back you, you won't be confronting the resistors with a moment of truth; they will be confronting you. To avoid this threat, you have to be vested with sufficient organizational power so that you can, if necessary, cut the resistors off.

When you have more time, your first priority is to develop influence by building change momentum. In taskforce change, widespread participation, or bottom-up initiatives, you do not have to deal with the resistors immediately, because, in the absence of an immediate threat, the resistors have less to focus on. Here you must mobilize the change agents, so the change vision can be clearly articulated and communicated to convince the bystanders to join in, and to get the change organization in place to give the traditionalists a new home. In the face of this momentum, the politics of influence largely takes care of itself; as we have seen in previous chapters, resistors have to convert, or be crowded out.

MONITORING THE BALANCE OF POWER BETWEEN CHANGE AGENTS AND RESISTORS

To monitor the balance of power, you have to note whether milestones are met and, in particular, whether the various players commit to the change (as a guide, you can use the steps for compact renewal outlined in the previous chapters). This means you have to have a clear sense of the change context, and a deep familiarity with the way momentum builds, or doesn't build, behind the unfolding effort.

At Delta Auto, the taskforce approach made sense, because time was available, but people were set in their ways and largely opposed change. The task forces did a credible job soliciting the input of the more successful dealers, country managers and head office people. Their early successes with the new dealer system in pilot projects confirmed that people were beginning to buy in. But then Continental began missing the milestones they had set for the roll out.

The change leadership team noticed a struggle emerging for influence between the change agents (successful dealers and young managers) who wanted to revise their compacts, and the resistors (sales and marketing people fearing a loss of power and the less successful dealers afraid of the new standards) who had no desire to revise their compacts. Both were competing for the allegiance of the traditionalists (old guard at head-office and country managers who were comfortable with the status quo and didn't want change) and remaining bystanders (senior management who were waiting to see

how things turned out and other country managers who could benefit but were not convinced the programme would work).

Sales and marketing people were raising more and more questions
about the appropriateness of the new standards, the main concern
being that the standards would take scarce time away from the selling
effort in the smaller dealers. As soon as the first questions were
resolved, new ones popped up. The less successful dealers rallied to
the cause calling for simplicity in place of what they saw as overly
complicated new procedures that would increase costs, but not sales.
Then the old guard at headquarters started calling for a review of the
whole process, to protect market share, they said. Something had to
be done to get the change process back on track.

TIMING INTERVENTION TO SHAPE THE POLITICS OF COMPACT RENEWAL

When you see a political pressure point and have the organizational
power to act, you have to decide how to deploy power and at what
speed. In the absence of strong change forces to justify the use of
power, the way you use your power can make a big difference to the
success of the change effort. Crudely used, power will create resent-
ment and a strong undercurrent of passive resistance.

No matter whether change is top down, or percolates spontaneously from the bottom up, there are several moments, or points, in
the change process when you have to bring power to bear, either as
change leader, or in support of the change leaders. The first is at the
beginning of the change process. You have to use influence and power,
if necessary, to open up the organization and get the change started.
Even in organizations that are already open to change, senior management sponsorship of the change effort is important early on.

At Delta Auto, despite the fact that people were largely against
change, some change agents emerged from the ranks of middle management to argue that the loyalty of the dealers was suffering, not

from a problem with the products, but from the nature of their relationships with the manufacturer. The change agents convinced top management to give them a mandate to improve the relationship. Without this sponsorship, they would not have been able to mobilize other change agents.

Your influence is also critical when the balance of power between change agents and resistors is tilting towards the latter. At Delta Auto, this was the point of increasing tension between the sales and marketing resistors and the young change agents. At this point, the senior management bystanders had the organizational power to withdraw support from, and kill, the change effort, or show their commitment to it. Fortunately for the change leaders, the successes of the change agents had impressed their senior colleagues. Senior management stepped in and offered the sales and marketing people a new compact they could not refuse. It included training in the skills needed to co-operate more closely with the dealers, and to implement the manufacturer's standards and the new dealer reward system, which had been designed to encourage a closer relationship.

The third point requiring your intervention is when a major commitment of resources is needed to pursue the change effort. At Delta Auto, this occurred immediately after the power balance between the change agents and the resistors had been corrected. Senior management had to commit to a new logistics system, company wide, to support more efficient delivery, as well as the new dealer reward system based on co-operative performance. And it had to put resources behind the skills training programme for the sales and marketing people, in order to change behaviour and transform the dealer relationship on the front line.

After the traditionalist old guard at head office and the traditionalists among the country managers saw which way the wind was blowing, they quickly inquired about joining the training programmes that had been developed to roll out the new dealer relationship. And once the traditionalists had joined the change process, the remaining resistors were effectively isolated. The resistors among the less successful dealers were left with the choice of either improving their performance by adopting the new standards, or dropping out of the dealer network, which some did. Over time, the new relationship with the manufacturer, plus the pruning of the dealer network, improved the average performance of the dealers dramatically.

Mastering the politics of compact renewal, the way top management did at Delta Auto, gives people the confidence to renew their compacts within the design of the current change effort. Once the process is well under way, you must prepare to build on the change already accomplished, on the first round of compact renewal, to move towards *ongoing change*. In Part III, you will see how to do this.

Part III

ONGOING
COMPACT
RENEWAL

The third step towards compacts for ongoing change is moving to employee-driven compact renewal. Chapter 13 shows you how to do so in terms of the four basic processes described in Part II. In Chapter 14, you will see how to develop a new social compact to support employee-driven change. Then, Chapter 15 will show you how to transform employee-driven change into ongoing change, by offering people learning compacts that encourage them to improve and innovate continually. To ensure that ongoing compact renewal creates maximum value in today's rapidly shifting economy, you will have periodically to reorient the focus of learning around the most relevant opportunities for value creation as shown in Chapter 16. Finally, Chapter 17 takes a brief look into the future to see how compact design and renewal will evolve with the spreading web of virtual business relationships.

MOVING TO
EMPLOYEE-DRIVEN
COMPACT RENEWAL

The best way to sustain front-line commitment is employee-driven compact renewal. Trying to strengthen commitment by piling on new initiatives from the top leads to confusion, lack of execution, and change overload on the front line. If you don't want your people to give mere lip service to new directives, put their heads down, and wait for the air to clear, you have to hand the initiative for change over to them. You have to make your employees responsible for deciding what the next change initiative should be on their level and for renewing their compacts themselves.

There are two basic channels for employee-driven compact renewal: innovation via bottom-up initiatives and/or efficiency improvement via widespread participation. In this chapter, we will show you how companies have moved to employee-driven compact renewal, starting with organizations that were closed to change. The process involves linking several of the basic change processes into a change path from top-down to bottom-up compact renewal. Closed organizations typically follow one of two classic paths: a discontinuous one that involves top-down turnaround and/or a continuous one that involves widespread participation. These are depicted in Figure 13.1.

On the discontinuous path (from task forces to top-down turnaround to bottom-up initiatives) it is difficult to get full front-line commitment. The pace of a top-down turnaround is so fast that, seen in terms of an organization's evolution, it amounts to a discontinuity, a giant step in the organization's development which leaves people with little time to adapt and buy in. By contrast, the continuous path from task forces to widespread participation to bottom-up initiatives, is more like a series of smaller steps, and lends itself more readily to the individual adaptation that is at the heart of full front-line commitment. We shall look at four examples that involve first, the discontinuous path and then, the continuous one:

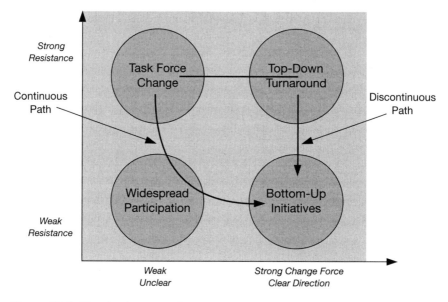

Figure 13.1 Classic change paths

- *Discontinuous path*
  - task forces to top-down turnaround
  - top-down turnaround to bottom-up initiatives.
- *Continuous path*
  - task forces to widespread participation
  - combining widespread participation with bottom-up initiatives.

DISCONTINUOUS PATH

From task forces to top-down turnaround

Have the task forces work rapidly with top management and then roll the change out in the form of a turnaround through the rest of the organization, rather than following the more time-consuming path of intensive solicitation of opinions, as in a pure taskforce approach. This is the classic process re-engineering approach. Whereas the task forces help shape the detail of their new compacts, the rest of the organization is presented with the new processes and related compacts as a *fait accompli*. This approach makes sense when top management needs the help of task forces to clarify the detailed direction of the change, with little time for intensive solicitation of opinions.

Key steps in the transition from task forces to top-down turnaround are:

- ask change agent task forces to work with top management to define change direction
- roll-out recommendations with top-down turnaround approach.

The disadvantage of turnaround change is that only the change agents can be mobilized with a positive psychological compact. If the change path stops after the top-down turnaround phase, it does not lead to employee-driven compact renewal. The new processes developed by the task forces require new ways of working. But top-down turnaround doesn't allow enough time, nor typically provide enough support, to develop new compacts that foster behavioural change. In such cases, fear drives the bystanders and traditionalists, who have a take-it-or-leave-it attitude and logic. They wait on the sidelines and watch how the change management deploys power to force resistors out. Under these conditions, you simply cannot ask people to take the initiative for compact renewal on the front line. You have to put in extra effort, as the following brief example illustrates, to get people on the front line to buy in.

The problem with process re-engineering at a retail bank

At one of Italy's larger retail banks with some 100 retail branches, re-engineering task forces redesigned both the front and back office processes. The new design took a lot of decision making away from the branch managers, and put it in the hands of tellers who had been retrained to provide an extended range of customer service, supported by new information systems. Once top management had approved the new design, the change leaders rolled it out in a wave process, with IT and transition management teams that washed through the branches, where people had little choice but to accept their new compacts, or leave. The branch managers, however, who wouldn't be easy to replace, began to find fault with the new processes. The whole re-engineering effort hung in the balance, until the managers' situation was addressed specifically with what was effectively a new economic compact, based not on front-line customer service by the branch managers, but on the integrated management of people and systems. Only after intensive discussion and training that went well beyond the top-down roll-out phase, did the branch managers begin to support, rather than try to control the tellers.

From top-down turnaround to bottom-up initiatives

Take advantage of the upheaval created by turnaround change to redesign the organization completely, opening it up for bottom-up initiatives by pushing decision making down to the front line, thereby making room for as many change agents and converted bystanders as possible. On the economic dimension, this involves converting sharply defined implementation compacts into decentralized entrepreneurial compacts and, on the social dimension, clearly building the flexibility needed for experimentation into the new rules of the game.

Key steps in the transition from top-down turnaround to bottom-up initiatives:

- force resistors out by making buy-in immediate
- radically decentralize to offer entrepreneurial compacts to change agents
- use the value-creating logic embodied in the new organization to convince as many bystanders as possible to convert to change agent compacts.

With this transition, you avoid the top-down cascaded assignments of a turnaround and, instead, challenge your change agents to develop new business opportunities; then, avoiding all or nothing offers to bystanders, you encourage them to follow the example of the change agents. The shift from turnaround to bottom-up initiatives, however, is limited typically to the change agents and converted bystanders. Not everyone can be a change agent. You will still be imposing a new organization on the traditionalists from the old organization, as in turnaround change, although it will take the form of new change agent-led teams. From the traditionalist point of view, the change looks very much like a top-down turnaround. And resistors still have to be forced out. Whatever ongoing compact renewal occurs, it will not involve everyone.

The Siemens Nixdorf shift from top-down turnaround to bottom-up initiatives

When Gerhard Schulmayer took over, Nixdorf was in crisis: annual losses of one billion Deutschmarks. In classic turnaround fashion, he started to replace and reconstitute the top management team with more than ten new managers, hired from some of the most entrepreneurial and successful companies in Europe. Still in turnaround mode, Schulmayer and the top team called together 100 plus top managers from around the company to design the new Nixdorf. The new decentralized organization marked the beginning of the shift towards change driven by bottom-up initiative.

Radical reorganization to provide room for entrepreneurial change agents

The new organization design was a loose matrix of 250 business units, each with a geographic, and a business line, focus. The business unit managers played a central role, with full responsibility for profit and loss. The overall business system, or value chain for each business, would vary depending on whether it was a product, service, or solutions business. The business unit managers would be the real decision makers; the geographic and business line managers sitting on the board of the business units would act only as sponsors and mentors. (This design was the same as that at ABB, the Swiss-Swedish engineering company where Schulmayer had previously headed the American operations.) Nixdorf offered prospective business unit managers entrepreneurial compacts to run and develop a unit.

To facilitate the transition to entrepreneurship, all prospective managers attended the 'Entrepreneurship Development Programme' run by faculty from three leading business schools. This highly interactive, action learning programme included a number of self-assessment exercises that culminated in a decision by the participants whether they were ready to take up the entrepreneurial challenge of business unit leadership. The 'Management Development Programme' also provided one week of training in business unit management skills to those who felt they could benefit. The training included techniques for diagnosing and optimizing business performance and managing a portfolio of businesses.

To measure performance, Nixdorf started using a standard financial management package for profit and loss accounting at the business unit level. Results went onto a balanced scorecard that included measures of customer and employee satisfaction. The company started assessing managers on both quantitative performance and qualitative behavioural factors, and aligned the new reward systems with these performance measures.

A critical phase in the transition from turnaround to bottom-up initiatives is to go beyond the inner circle of change agents managing the business units, to get change agents wherever they may be to come forward with their projects. To encourage the development of new business ideas through experimentation and entrepreneurship, Schulmayer and his team launched an 'Innovation Initiative'. Top management created an internal venture capital fund to which prospective entrepreneurs could appeal for funding outside their business units. In addition, they had access to entrepreneurial competence throughout the company via a data bank of individual expertise. This meant that someone with a product, service, or solutions idea, but no marketing or financial know-how, could get the help needed to put together a business plan.

To create a supportive environment for innovation and entrepreneurship, the Siemens Nixdorf management formed work groups in lines of business across the company to encourage the discussion of business issues and the exchange of best entrepreneurial practice. In particular, monthly 'Friday Forums' provided forums for exchanging success stories and problems, and facilitating the access to expertise. In the same vein, people went on external benchmarking visits to companies known for their innovation, including several in Silicon Valley. But the most significant support for entrepreneurial compacts came from the effort to convert hundreds of employee bystanders into change agents.

Extending the entrepreneurial effort by convincing bystanders to become change agents

The change leadership organized four events in Hanover, Germany, between late 1994 and 1996, each time inviting 300 to 400 different employees who were interested in the change process. At these meetings, particular stakeholder groups shared their views about the corporate transformation and set up action teams to integrate them into the process. The theme of Hanover I was 'The voice of the employees'. It gave participants the opportunity to discuss the new values and informal rules needed to make Siemens Nixdorf an entrepreneurial company: 59 action teams were formed. Each agreed to a compact to produce some results within 90 days and a substantial value-creating impact inside of 180 days. Hanover II focused on 'The voice of the customers'; 54 key clients attended a meeting of 350 employees to discuss what customers expected of the company. Some participated in the 20 action teams set up to address customer issues. Hanover III was on 'The voice of the partners'; 40 suppliers and distributors joined several hundred employees to raise partner issues and join the related action teams. Finally, Hanover IV was on 'Institutionalizing the capability to change'; some 400 employees looked at ways of taking the output from the first three events and making it part of the ongoing life of the company.

The challenge for the action teams from the last event was how to take proposals from what were essentially off-line task forces with a temporary mandate, and integrate them into the company's ongoing on-line activity. Among the proposals were new forms of communication based on the company's Intranet to encourage co-operation across the business units. But here they ran into the limits imposed by the independent nature of bottom-up entrepreneurial activity. The communication took place, but co-operation was more difficult to implement. With each business unit and new venture responsible primarily for its own bottom line, people were happy to give lip service to co-operation and new proposals as long as it didn't cost them anything.

Yet, the transformation at Siemens Nixdorf has, after all, created impressive bottom-up initiatives at the level of the business unit managers, as well as an ongoing series of one-time initiatives by employees with new venture ideas. It is important to note that these change agents had explicit new compacts to initiate change based on their business unit, or new venture plans. However, many employees were still not part of employee-driven change. Nevertheless, by the end of 1996, the company had come back dramatically from several years of hundreds of million Deutschmark annual losses, to break even, with numerous new products, several of them on the Internet, and a greatly improved market image.

CONTINUOUS PATH

From task forces to widespread participation

The problem with taskforce change is that, even when properly executed with intensive solicitation of opinions throughout the organization, it remains a top-down process. As long as the initiative for change only comes from the top, you cannot expect employee-driven compact renewal on the front line. In addition, the temptation is great for top management to get impatient with the pace of the taskforce consultation process and switch to top-down turnaround, which makes it even less likely to get employee-driven compact renewal on the front line.

Shift from taskforce change to widespread participation by broadening the solicitation of opinion by taskforces, into collaborative dialogue with bystanders and the relatively isolated work of taskforce implementation groups, into the widespread integrated teamwork that draws traditionalists into participative change. On the economic dimension, you have to generalize the special compacts of the design task force to new compacts that make everyone responsible for change throughout the organization; on the social dimension, you need to build on individual information sharing to get the full involvement of people in teams taking the initiative for change. You also need additional change agents, not only the task-oriented types who can design new processes, but also the people-oriented ones who can help others work in integrated teams. And, since the heavy resistors presumably have been crowded out during the taskforce phase, you can convert other potential resistors during the participative phase by increasing team pressure from their peers.

The key steps in the transition from taskforce change to widespread participation:

- follow taskforce recommendations by collaborative dialogue with bystanders
- integrate the participative effort with teamwork to involve traditionalists
- get a widespread commitment to action.

The Global Business Communication Systems shift from taskforce change to widespread participation

Jerre Stead, the new chief executive of AT&T Global Business Communication Systems (GBCS), transformed the re-engineering effort into participative change just before AT&T was split up in 1996. The taskforce change started with a standard re-engineering effort in what was then the BCS business unit, to stem the loss of money, declining sales, low customer satisfaction, and even lower employee satisfaction. The then president of the business unit put together a 25-person, cross-functional team of external consultants and internal change agents to examine current processes and define a more profitable way of operating. The pilot test of the new order fulfilment process led to new job responsibilities, skill requirements, and training, as well as an augmented IT system. IT teams, process teams, and local transition management teams supported the roll out of the new process through the 20 offices of the business unit, each with roughly one hundred people.

Jerre Stead took over during the roll out. His mandate? Merge the BCS unit with another one to form the GBCS division. Although evidence of success in the pilot projects was increasing (cycle time was cut from three months to three weeks and costs by 30 per cent), he noticed that the change leadership was using mainly a turnaround, take-it-or-leave-it approach to bringing people in the offices on board. His sense was that there was little change in the minds and attitudes of employees, nor in what he called the 'cultural processes'. To deepen and spread the individual change, Stead started working on the social dimension first, then on the economic dimension.

Moving from taskforce recommendations to collaborative dialogue with bystanders

With the intent of moving beyond the technicalities of re-engineering to new values and behaviour, Stead ran a series of workshops to formulate a mission, vision, values, and objectives with the top executives. These workshops were run in a top-down way, but based on the principle of dialogue between equals. The workshops came up with the following mission: 'To be the world leader in providing the highest quality business communication products, services, and solutions'. This statement defined the obvious focus of the business. The vision was 'To be your partner of choice: dedicated to quality, committed to your success', a statement of intent to provide customer value through quality products and partnership. The group came up with seven key values, each backed up by a short supporting statement: 'Respect for individuals, dedication to helping customers, highest standards of integrity, innovation, teamwork, accountability, and excellence'.

As value statements go, this was rather standard. However, after the organization had been delayered from 14 levels to five, the values were systematically cascaded down through to the front line. In some meetings, 80 per cent of the time was spent discussing the values and how they apply. According to one insider:

> 'There's an incredible emphasis at the top of this business on our values – orders of magnitude more than I have experienced – and in penetrating emotional depth, not just intellectual. Right now we're one of the most de-politicized organizations around, and it's because we share a vision.'

Each business put together its own adapted version of the values statement. Managers specified their objectives in the form of a 'value equation' which described how their plans would both embody the core values and contribute to associates' satisfaction and/or customer satisfaction and/or shareholder wealth. In so doing, the managers were made to take more initiative for change, within the social compact embodied in the value equation.

Integrating the participative effort with widespread teamwork

Extensive training helped managers become coaches, people-oriented change agents who could help employees understand the value equation and how they could add value to the processes as members of the team in each office. To integrate the effort vertically across the levels in the organization, several new means of communication helped people understand what top management was getting at. 'Ask the President' provided a 48-hour response to questions that employees wrote or called in. 'The Answer Line' was an 0800 number employees could call to get information or questions answered by a relevant subject expert. 'Chats' was the name given to the regular informal discussions which Stead held with small groups of employees. 'All Associate Broadcasts' referred to the quarterly interactive video broadcast on the application of values with live call-in questions and an audio recording for subsequent information requests.

To integrate the effort horizontally across the offices in the business, the Human Resources group at GBCS organized several co-ordination teams. The 'Associate Services Team' administered salaries, the recognition schemes, employee surveys, and provided advice on all related issues. The 'Education and Training Team' delivered leadership and technical training to support the new values and rules of the game. 'The Labour Planning Team' prepared employees for assignments with self-managing teams and new technology, thereby helping to ensure good relationships with the unions. The 'Diversity Planning Team' promoted respect for individuals by providing advice, counselling, and seminars on how to understand and work with all types of people. And finally, the 'Associate Communications Team' managed the employee communication channels mentioned above.

Getting a widespread commitment to action

Stead asked Fred Lane to head up the Human Resources organization and help him implement 'Performance Excellence Partnerships', compacts designed to encourage everyone to take the initiative for personal change. These compacts with individuals helped them fully develop their talent, based on an individual process for setting and monitoring SMART (Specific, Measurable, Achievable, Relevant, Timely) objectives, together with tri-annual monitoring and feedback. As part of this process, individuals planned their own training to improve both personal and team performance.

In terms of performance appraisal, the compacts of the managers included the annual 360-degree feedback introduced by the CEO of AT&T, Bob Allen, and adopted by GCBS. After a survey in 1991 showed that only 19 per cent of AT&T employees believed statements by top managers, Allen had started the process, getting himself evaluated by his team and reporting the outcome to the board. He then asked his team to have themselves rated by their subordinates and by one another, and so on down through the organization.

The economic reward built into these new compacts at GBCS included two new bonus schemes, the Profit Sharing Plan (PSP) and the Special Long-Term Plan (SLTP). PSP was aimed at middle managers and associates who participated in profit gains if they met customer satisfaction and financial targets. The individual annual performance review looked at both the individual achievement of objectives, relative to associate, customer, and shareholder value where appropriate, and the extent to which individual behaviour reflected the divisional values statement. SLTP was for senior managers, based on PSP, but also reflecting the improvement in associate satisfaction and an averaging formula to ensure that short-term gains did not drive out long-term improvement. This measurement and reward system explicitly shared gains; it encouraged everyone to renew their compacts continually in line with evolving objectives of the change.

The results of the change effort at GBCS suggest that the effort was successful. Over the four years from 1989 to 1993, while 19 000 of the 26 000 employees changed the content of their jobs, extreme employee satisfaction increased from 38 per cent to 63 per cent. During the same period, customer satisfaction went up from 53 per cent to 80 per cent and projects management satisfaction from 41 per cent to 90 per cent. Most important, revenues increased, costs were cut, and GBCS had its first profitable year in 1993. What is unclear at the time of writing, however, is how the ongoing downsizing after the break-up of the old AT&T is affecting employee-driven change in the new companies; informal reports suggest that people on the front line are suffering from change fatigue.

Combining widespread participation with bottom-up initiatives

The problem with participative improvement is that employees are restricted in their initiatives to what their existing team is willing to undertake. On the other hand, the limitation of bottom-up initiatives is that the initiative for change is restricted to change agents and converted bystanders. What one would like is employee-driven compact renewal that encompasses both the widespread improvement associated with participative change and the innovation that emerges from bottom-up initiatives. However, combining widespread participation with bottom-up initiatives is more easily said than done. The former requires that employees immerse themselves in a team effort following prescribed rules of the game, whereas the latter is driven first by individual initiative and only then by a team that forms around the internal entrepreneur.

Combine widespread participation with bottom-up initiatives by loosening the rules of the participative game to encourage the emergence of intrapreneurs. The path to a combination of widespread improvement with bottom-up initiatives starts more naturally with the former. Observation of successful practice suggests that going in the other direction, trying to nurture the discipline of participative integration across bottom-up initiatives, tends to stifle the latter.

The key steps in the combination of widespread participation with bottom-up initiatives are the following:

- Involve bystanders in widespread dialogue to define the change.
- Lock in a commitment to action in the context of widespread teamwork.
- Call for bottom-up initiatives within specific value-creating guidelines with the necessary support for experimentation.
- Loosen the guidelines further to encourage wider ranging innovation initiatives when the external change drivers become clearer.

The IBM Customer Services' use of widespread participation and bottom-up initiatives

To see how this can be done, let's look at an IBM example of the integration of customer services across several countries. IBM had a history of strong country organizations around the world. The move to global lines of business demanded the integration of activities across countries, with all the usual resistance that such a shift generates in the country kingdoms. The story here is about the alignment of the customer services in a particular region across four countries. The services comprised consulting, outsourcing, software solutions, and support services; some 1500 people were involved in the countries concerned. The new regional vice-president of services started a participative process, because he didn't have the authority to do much else. Fortunately for him, IBM had been through so much change by that time that people expected to be involved in any important moves. In addition, it wasn't clear how integration was supposed to be implemented across the countries, so all in all, a participative approach made sense. The vice-president began by visiting the people reporting to him in the countries to put together a change management leadership team, with a member from each country to help build the new customer service teams and manage the change there.

Involving people in collaborative dialogue to define the change

The vice-president started a first round of discussions to familiarize people with the need for, and nature of, the change. 'The first thing was to build a personal relation with the people, to develop a bridge that would generate some trust. It took time. It is one thing to go there and deliver a nice speech. It is another to get the people to open up and listen.' Everybody was very polite, but nothing much happened. A big problem was bringing the general guidelines for the new IBM global services organization down to earth and adapting them to the local conditions with very different size scales and working cultures. The new matrix structure meant that the number of key managers would more than double, unless the structure was adapted to the different local situations.

Despite innumerable discussions about structure and the customer relations process, the new process teams were not functioning with the energy the vice-president was looking for: 'I can have very nice charts to show you that everything is running fine, but the real action hasn't occurred yet'. To find out what was going on, the vice-president held informal meetings over breakfast and lunch. People only really opened up when he began to address the question, 'What's in it for us?'

> 'During the first two to three months, we had a very formal reaction, until we gave some signs of real support for their projects. The loan of key resources they needed, consulting people, information technology architects, some key programmers, or analysts. That was the only way they could test that we meant what we were saying about co-operation.'

Once they began to see that the new rules of the game could work in their favour, the process teams began to coalesce around the change agents.

Locking in a commitment to action within the context of widespread teamwork

The real shift from a country to a line of service commitment, for everyone, including the traditionalists, came with the renewal of people's compacts, what IBM calls the 'Personal Business Commitments'. These involve a very simple, short, written personal statement in which individuals translate their business unit's or manager's objectives, into supporting personal objectives on three dimensions:

- a quantitative dimension in the form of revenue, profit, and customer satisfaction goals
- a people dimension in the form of teamwork objectives
- an execution dimension in the form of an action plan that includes training and personal development.

The compacts are supported by the usual range of IBM training programs and promotion ladders, plus performance evaluation on a scale of one to three on each dimension.

To align the new compacts with the lines of business, the vice-president tied the 30 per cent variable component of the compensation package to the regional performance on the three quantitative factors (revenue, gross profit, and customer satisfaction). Special attention was focused on objectives and actions aimed at ongoing improvement in the process teams.

166

'The buy-in of people comes not only from the deployment of some tool and some meetings, saying OK we will start to use this process. I believe that processes take some time to really be part of your everyday activities.'

A straightforward cascading approach was employed to renew the compacts. The vice-president developed his budget and action plan with his team and asked them to translate it into budgets for their business units, together with their personal objectives, and so on down to the front line. These formed the basis of each employee's written Personal Business Commitment, which was discussed individually with the boss and signed by both parties. According to the vice-president, this somewhat formal procedure was essential to avoid confusion across the languages and cultures of the different country organizations. What it did was put the initiative for action and process improvement across the countries in the hands of every customer services employee.

It is important to remember, however, that such formal commitments, to be really effective, need a psychological and social dimension. In the words of the vice-president:

'The formal piece of this process will not be of such a great help if you do not have the psychological commitment of the people. You have to go beyond the formal relation you have in any business to build some kind of human relationship. You have to share things that go beyond the business, while being very careful not to invade a person's privacy, being sensitive to different personalities.'

Opening up for bottom-up initiatives

With the new line-of-service process teams up and running, the management team had to confront a number of issues that were not being resolved within the continual improvement framework. At his breakfast meetings with the unit heads, the vice-president put these so-called key issues on the table and asked people to call for ideas directly from the front line. People with ideas were asked to flesh them out first, to explore the idea to see if they could get some results:

'Don't come to me if you have ideas or solutions, go ahead and do it. Try it out, and then once you have figured out if it works or not, then come to us. If you need resources or you need decisions, we will try to help you.'

In the first six months, there were 20 to 25 ideas that reached the experimental project stage and 12 that matured into 'projects of significance'.

The reason people on the front line responded so well to this simple call for initiatives was that they too perceived the limitations of participative improvement in responding to complex customer requests that required creative new solutions. The Personal Business Commitment had opened them up to taking the initiative, and many wanted to go beyond incremental change. At the time of writing, the pace of change, market and technological development, in several of IBM's business segments has accelerated so much that there is less and less time for incremental participative change. Business unit leaders are being encouraged to move into action and execute as rapidly as possible. In the words of one vice-president in charge of solutions software, 'Those who can't keep up have to get out of the way.'

IMPLICATIONS FOR ONGOING COMPACT RENEWAL

No matter what the path taken to employee-driven change, it only works if employees have a compact that encourages them to take the initiative on compact renewal. The examples in this chapter make the point. In the case of Siemens-Nixdorf, it was the entrepreneurial compacts of the business unit managers; in the case of GBCS, it was the Performance Excellence Partnerships; in the case of IBM customer services, it was the Personal Business Commitments. However, if employees are going to drive front-line commitment, not on a one-off basis, but repeatedly, they need a social compact that supports employee-driven change.

DEVELOPING A SOCIAL COMPACT FOR EMPLOYEE-DRIVEN CHANGE

If employee-driven change is not to peter out, you have to go beyond the original change processes and create a context for continual compact renewal. While employees can initiate compact renewal on their own, if the effect is to be durable and organization-wide, you have to provide the right context. Taking the initiative for continual compact renewal is all about understanding and being motivated to make the next move.

This context cannot be created in a vacuum. It has to be developed on the foundation provided by the previous change processes. Unfortunately, the social compact associated with previous change is often inimical to what is needed for continual compact renewal on the front line. Putting in place a social compact for employee-driven change that lasts, therefore, demands a sensitivity to what is already in place and an approach to altering it.

BRITISH NUCLEAR FUELS: ESSENTIAL FOUNDATIONS OF A NEW SOCIAL COMPACT

There are two essential foundations for a new social compact that supports employee-driven change:

- an open-ended value-creating framework for what to do next
- corresponding values and rules on how to make the next individual move.

Employee-driven change creates multiple, overlapping change agendas. To avoid confusion on the front line, a coherent value-creating framework, backed up by supporting values and rules of the game, is essential. The starting point is the first round of compact renewal described in Parts I and II. If the first rounds are done properly, all the players will have redesigned their compacts to support the overall value-creating idea. When the value-creating framework is open-ended enough, the players will have a shared understanding of how value can be created in the future. If not, the process fizzles out.

The need for an open-ended value-creating framework for what to do next

British Nuclear Fuels Plc (which enriches uranium, manufactures nuclear reactor fuel, operates a nuclear power plant, and disposes of spent fuel) introduced numerous change and improvement initiatives in the eighties to move employees towards bottom-up compact renewal: Quality Circles, Team Briefing, Attitude Surveys, Zero-Based Budgeting, Effective Resource Management, Value Engineering, and so on. When management decided to focus on 'improving the change and improvement process we already had in place' they interviewed hundreds of employees on all levels to find out what they thought about the process of ongoing change.

The interviews of employees revealed that:

> 'many of our people were unclear about their own role in the improvement process, including many of our managers. Giving people training and then expecting them to bring about change and improvement just because you have told them they are "empowered" does not work.'

Management found that ongoing change had been cut off by the lack of a clear value-creating framework within which individuals can take the initiative for compact renewal.

Moving towards such a framework, top management introduced a conventional 'strategic management process' focused on the relationship between headquarters and the operating units. A 'contract' between the two sides embodied this relationship. Headquarters provided the operating units with the 'company strategic plan', including mission, vision, values, objectives, and targets, while the operating units formulated their own 'strategic plan/business plan', including an 'environmental assessment' of threats and opportunities. 'Once plans and targets have been agreed they form a contract between the divisions and headquarters. This contract limits the amount of interference from above and empowers managers to get on and manage their business.'

The basic value-creating framework, embodied in the Strategic Management Process, was essential to aligning the different economic compacts of individuals. With this in mind, British Nuclear Fuels has opened the business planning process to as many people as possible, to ensure that compacts throughout the organization are consistent with overall corporate objectives. In addition, cross-divisional project groups have been put in place to focus the strategic direction of the company on the major market segments. This has helped clarify people's understanding of the direction in which they should be moving and, in particular, the kind of front-line change needed to create value for the company.

The need for shared values and rules on how to make the next move

Trust is the second essential pre-condition for lasting employee-driven change. To open up enough to change their ways, to adapt and experiment, employees must be totally confident that management will not manipulate them in the process. Taking the initiative for compact renewal requires a willingness to be wrong, hence the absolute necessity for a shared sense that one's own initiative will be based on the same values as everyone else.

At British Nuclear Fuels, management found that the lack of a shared set of values and rules had blocked ongoing change. Only a small proportion of the people had really been involved in the various change efforts so far. Many blue collar workers felt left out, and many first-line and middle-line managers felt the improvement teams were a threat, because they were not included. Moreover, the teams dealt with problems of *their* choice rather than those that the managers set as a priority. There was little sign of cross-functional or cross-departmental activity, while real communication with customers and suppliers only occurred when there was a conflict. In addition, people said there was too much of a 'blame and fear' culture with too many managers exhibiting a command and control, 'attack/defence' style. Senior managers were perceived to be short term in their thinking, with a tendency towards the latest 'flavour of the month'.

Top management realized that there was a huge gap between the employee-driven change they thought they had been encouraging and what was actually happening on the ground. There was no sense of shared values and rules of the game. Rather, the fragmented approach to the introduction of new change and improvement initiatives had led to a climate of scepticism and insecurity. Moreover, the management style on all levels was 'far too directive ... when we needed a style which encouraged our people to continually develop better ways of conducting the business'. With this in mind, they started a large education programme at the top cascading down, which focused on style, together with structured problem-solving and prevention techniques, so that everyone would be exposed to a common set of values, concepts, and tools.

The British Nuclear Fuels experience illustrates how illusory it is to talk about employee-driven change without a shared sense of what is to be created and how. The change processes fell far short of what management had in mind. To put employee-driven change back on track, they had to move towards a coherent, open-ended framework for creating economic value supported by shared values and rules.

GENERAL ELECTRIC: MOVING FROM AN OLD SOCIAL COMPACT TO A NEW ONE

Developing shared values and rules to support ongoing change is much more easily said than done, owing to the confusion in values created moving from one change process to another. The main problem is the interference from old values, formal and informal rules. One of the best examples of the pitfalls is provided by the most widely

174

and intensively studied management case over the last two decades, namely, Jack Welch's leadership of General Electric.

Shortly after taking the helm at GE, Welch had identified the values he believed were key to being number one or two in each market. These values were laid out in the GE Value Statement at that time and can be summarized as follows:

- lean and agile
- ownership
- entrepreneurship
- stewardship (coaching of employees)
- quality and excellence
- reality and candour
- open communications.

After seven years of downsizing, delayering, and restructuring (what we shall simply call 'turnaround') that came to an end with the RCA acquisition in the late eighties, Welch was frustrated by the lack of initiative among his managers. Although the objectives were sharply focused on being number one or two in the industry, although organization layers had been peeled away, the corporate staff made much leaner, in a support rather than control mode, the planning process simplified to concentrate on the business rather than documents, and managers rewarded for producing superior financial results, Welch believed GE managers were not living out the new values, particularly, entrepreneurship, empowerment of employees, openness to partnership with customers and suppliers across the boundaries of the company. A typical response was that relying on people and ideas was: 'fine until some of those people make big mistakes. Then we will miss having those systematic plans'.

The gap between espoused and actual values and rules was due to the way top-down turnaround had reinforced GE's traditional culture, to the detriment of the new values needed for lasting employee-driven change.

Interference from old values

Under the previous CEO, Reginald Jones, an individualistic, power-oriented approach characterized GE, which was, after all, typical of American corporate life of the time. Jones had reorganized to clarify responsibilities. GE had had strategic business units (SBUs) for strategic planning and departments to run operations. Jones eliminated this confusing double structure: he abolished the departments and integrated planning and operations in the SBUs. So, the SBU managers took on more power and authority. Later on, when Welch delayered GE, he cut costs, but he also reinforced the power of the SBU managers. Although bureaucracy was reduced, managers were no more willing than they had been to reduce the power distance between themselves and their subordinates, especially in the face of the need to protect themselves during the downsizing. Against this backdrop, Welch's call for more stewardship and coaching, for example, was not very credible.

Welch inherited risk-aversion from the Jones era: the highly structured, methodological planning system had systematically discouraged GE managers from taking unplanned risks. But since risks cannot be readily planned, the system effectively discouraged mangers from taking any risks at all. Welch wanted his managers to take more initiative and risk, to be willing and open to empowering their subordinates. However, by calling for more entrepreneurship in GE managers' actions, Welch pitted himself not only against GE's risk-averse heritage, but also the uncertainty he himself had generated with the downsizing.

During the turnaround phase, with all the layoffs, it was only natural for GE people to avoid any risks that might jeopardize their position. Welch's almost evangelical drive to turn the company around, and his low tolerance for softer, less action-oriented people, caused others to perceive him as 'yelling and screaming for performance'. No wonder GE managers backed away from risk.

Interference from old formal rules

In terms of formal organization, GE had been very hierarchical, with individually-oriented, boss-subordinate relationships.

Sector Executives reviewed and controlled SBU plans, while the Corporate Executive Office controlled the Sector Executives. This was common in US companies at the time. Practising managers in larger companies still managed their subordinates according to the traditional military model of command and control. Only a few academics and consultants really accepted the notion of empowerment.

During the turnaround phase, Welch reduced the number of management levels from nine on average to four, and the number of jobs in the company by 25 per cent, weeding people out on the basis of individual performance. When he later called for more teamwork to take advantage of all the talent in the company, and exhorted his managers to share information and be open with their people, he ran up against individually-based values and rules that reflected people's needs to save their own skins, a need that had been deeply ingrained during the turnaround.

Compensation at GE had been based primarily on position. People tended to protect their reputations and avoid taking the blame for failure. When Welch demanded that people take more responsibility for results and then linked rewards much more strongly to performance, he was challenging the GE approach from the Jones era. Moreover, the uncertainty created by the restructuring forced everyone to look after themselves, to make sure that they were credited with success, not associated with failure. This meant that people had to manage their performance image. So instead of real performance, image and reputation also remained key to success.

Interference from old informal rules

To stimulate more entrepreneurship and empowerment, Welch expected his managers to coach, not confront, and inspire, not control. However, Welch's his own style during the turnaround had been confrontational:

> 'You can't even say hello to Jack without it being confrontational. If you don't want to step up to Jack toe-to-toe, belly-to-belly, and argue your point, he doesn't have use for you.'

Thus, the simplification in planning and control procedures was overshadowed by the confrontational style, which in turn, turned off many of those who might otherwise have taken a more nurturing approach to management.

In brief, after the RCA acquisition, the rules and values inherited from the Jones era and reinforced during the turnaround, clashed with Welch's new objectives. The call for more sharing, openness and coaching, had little real precedent in the experience of GE managers. Prevailing social compacts do not yield easily to exhortation.

3M VS. GE: IMPLANTING A SOCIAL COMPACT FOR EMPLOYEE-DRIVEN CHANGE

At the core of the social compact for employee-driven change, beyond the shared value-creating framework, is the bond of trust that unites management and the employees in a shared, continual renewal. In the words of Jack Welch:

> 'Trust is enormously powerful in a corporation. People won't do their best unless they believe they'll be treated fairly – that there's no cronyism and everybody has a real shot. The only way I know to create that trust is by laying out your values and then walking the talk. You've got to do what you say you'll do, consistently, over time.'

To install values and rules for employee-driven change:

- champion and reward experimentation and initiative
- stimulate intensive communication across boundaries
- provide easy access to necessary resources.

Putting these values and rules in place requires sustained effort over many years. 3M is one of the companies that has gone the farthest in stimulating ongoing bottom-up change, in the form of innovation. The 3M effort, notable for its longevity and consistency, highlights the importance of sustaining these values over time.

Championing and rewarding experimentation and initiative

The 3M mission statement enshrines bottom-up initiative. Entrepreneurship is its number one business principle:

> 'Our first business principle is the promotion of entrepreneurship and insistence upon freedom in the workplace to pursue innovative ideas. Policies, practices and organization structure are flexible and characterized by mutual trust and co-operation.'

Already in 1948, the then CEO, McKnight, developed a set of principles to encourage innovation and individual initiative. Among them was 'Allow an employee to take a risk and give him/her your full support'. Following this principle, the famous '30% Challenge' (that 30% of sales come from new products introduced over the last four years) has become a corporate standard. According to the current CEO, Livio DeSimone, 'Innovation tells us where to go; we don't tell innovation where to go'.

In 1963, the Carlton Society was established to honour extraordinary scientific and technical contributions at 3M. An abundance of stories and quotes describe major innovations: 'We were determined to make it work. We hit roadblocks, but we said, "Let's run more experiments".' Two large sections of the 3M Internet site are devoted to its innovative activity. But the company goes way beyond recognition to reward initiative and performance among researchers, the sales staff, and other professionals. Its Dual Ladder System provides non-managerial employees with a career ladder identical to management in prestige, position, and compensation.

At GE, Welch also has insisted that recognition and rewards go to managers who take initiative to produce superior results and that honest failures be protected:

> 'We want to give big rewards to those who do things, but without going after the scalps of those who reach for the big but fail. Punishing failure assures that no one dares.'

Welch moved vigorously to promote those who not only delivered on their hard commitments, but were also living up to the values of the company: 'We cannot afford management styles that suppress and intimidate'. For those who produced results, bonuses of 30–40 per cent were common, with salary increases of 10–15 per cent accompanied by stock options.

Stimulating intensive communication across boundaries

The 3M management actively encourages its people to share technology and best practice. Already in 1951, the company established the 3M Technical Forum to 'encourage free and active interchange of information and cross-fertilization of ideas'. The Leading Edge Academic Programme provides funding for members of the 3M technical community to collaborate on advanced technical work at government laboratories and academic institutions. Educational programmes, chapter meetings, symposia, and international teamwork spread ideas around the company. A breakthrough in one field is rapidly exploited in other areas, for example, micro-replication research on overhead projector lenses was incorporated in new structural abrasives, lighting products, LCD displays, fibre optic connectors, and better computer mouse pads.

At 3M, customers are the other critical source of ideas and information. The company observes them using 3M products, monitors their response in test markets, solicits their comments in focus groups, with reply cards, and so on. Numerous 3M innovation projects have turned to customers for guidance when they ran into dead-ends or obstacles. 3M expects its sales people to hang around its customers with an eye for product development opportunities. According to 3M, each of its 60 000 products was developed in response to a customer need.

At GE, Welch has promoted a 'boundaryless' organization by removing the barriers between different groups in the company, especially between the company and its customers and suppliers. Removing the barriers meant exposing people to the natural forces of control in the form of direct contact with their customers, suppliers, and partners, both inside and outside the company. Welch used a 'Change Acceleration Process' process to encourage cross-functional project teams and partnerships, both within and across corporate boundaries. In this new environment, he sought leaders who 'walked the talk'. Only those who had the self-confidence to trust and empower others could themselves be trusted.

At GE, to get managers to listen to their people, Welch and the Crotonville management development director, Jim Baughman, designed the famous GE Work-Out sessions, open forums for frank discussion of employee proposals for change. Managers had to say yes or no immediately to proposals, or give a decision within a month. About 700 sessions were held annually throughout GE, covering not only business unit activities and processes, but also cross-functional responsibilities, and relationships with suppliers and customers. In the first two years, the company acted on 90 per cent of the suggested operational improvements, concrete evidence of the value management attached to the opinions of GE employees.

Providing easy access to the necessary resources

At 3M there are numerous conduits to resources for new initiatives beyond one's immediate superior. Most prominent is the 15 per cent Rule, whereby people can spend 15 per cent of their time exclusively on projects of their own choice. Spending slack time and resources on new initiatives run in parallel with people's mainstream activities, also known as 'bootlegging', is one of the most widely touted sources of 3M innovation. As one pilot plant manager put it: 'If you have any weird ideas that wouldn't upset production or require large expenditure, go ahead'.

Beyond the 15 per cent Rule, more formal funding channels for new initiatives exist: employees can apply for 3M Genesis Grants to take promising research beyond the idea stage. The 3M Pacing Plus Program, which sets worldwide priorities and provides laboratory resources and financial funding for high potential product initiatives, co-ordinates the portfolio of new initiatives in the development phase throughout the company. The multiple resource channels allow product champions to pursue a new idea for years. The total time from idea start-up to product commercialization is often five to ten years, and can involve ten different 3M laboratories bringing together highly diverse expertise.

At GE the Change Acceleration Process (CAP) was designed to 'accelerate Work-Out self-sufficiency efforts, transfer best practices around leading change, and enhance the capabilities of GE leaders to initiate and lead change efforts'. In the first two years, about 740 people in 64 change project teams went through the CAP process, 50 internal coaches were trained, and several divisions started to internalize the process, with special attention to customer- and partner-related issues. The CAP and Work-Out efforts gave front-line people access to the tools and resources for ongoing change initiatives designed to enhance speed and globalization, improve processes, adopt best practices from inside and outside, empower people to 'bust bureaucracy', and move into action.

THE DIFFERENCE BETWEEN THE SOCIAL COMPACTS
AT 3M AND GE

The contrasts between the 3M and GE approaches highlight the differences in their social compacts. 3M has a growth network based on a continual stream of bottom-up product initiatives from people on the front line; GE relies mainly on its business unit managers for growth initatives.

It is no accident that 3M is so innovative and has received so many accolades over the years. Innovation is deeply ingrained in the culture, supported by formal rules of the game and a long-standing social compact of informal rules and values. According to William Coyne, the head of R&D, the reason creative people stay with the company rather than leave and found their own firms, 'is not money or fame, but the chance to play again. If you are the kind of person who loves to innovate, nothing is more desirable'. This social compact stimulates employee-driven innovation. A key feature is the motivation people have on the front line to innovate and learn.

GE, by contrast, has pushed for employee-driven initiatives on the business unit managerial level. This is confirmed by the fact that, in order to maintain high shareholder returns in the late nineties, Jack Welch has been forced to launch yet another round of downsizing. Although Welch has talked about 'changing the relationship between the boss and his subordinates' to empower the latter, the people on the front line evidently haven't been generating enough value to justify their existence. Otherwise, why would they be cut? This raises a question. To what extent does the change at GE reflect the energy and drive of the CEO, and his top management, as opposed to the ability of the lower level managers and people on the front line to learn and sustain the effort themselves?

Whereas at 3M employee-driven change creates continual value, at GE the input of the CEO is relatively more important. At 3M, in contrast to GE, people on the front line are apparently able to learn and sustain the effort themselves. At 3M, there is also much more organizational infrastructure in place to support front-line learning. This suggests that, to transform employee-driven change into ongoing change on the front line, you have to go beyond a new social compact and offer individuals the organizational support for learning-based compacts.

NURTURING LEARNING COMPACTS FOR ONGOING CHANGE

Managers and employees who learn to innovate continually, or improve on what they are doing, have learning compacts. They are updating and changing their compacts on their own initiative, not once, but repeatedly. On the economic dimension, they continually look for new and better ways of doing things, adapting to, anticipating, and possibly shaping their business environment; on the social dimension, they prefer values and rules that promote continual individual and team change; on the psychological dimension, they get satisfaction from the personal development in such learning.

Once your employees are driving compact renewal, supported by a social compact for employee-driven change, you have the opportunity to create a more anticipatory, creative organization by installing learning compacts. We are not concerned here with one-time efficiency improvement, or a single innovation, but with ongoing, self-driven compact renewal that creates a stream of efficiency improvements and innovations on the front line, which your company can deploy to outpace the competition. But you have to put in place the right enabling processes to help your people build into their compacts a process of ongoing learning about the business. Before seeing how this can be done, let us look at examples of learning compacts.

TWO TYPES OF LEARNING COMPACT ON THE FRONT LINE

There are two types of learning compact:

- efficiency-based
- innovation-based.

Efficiency learning compacts require employees to commit themselves explicitly to participate in ongoing compact renewal continually to improve the way things are done and, thereby, cut costs. Employees agree to learn how to look continually for better ways of doing things and change their working methods, while the company gives them the climate, training, logistical support, and recognition needed to make improvement attractive. Successful examples of ongoing widespread problem-solving exist, even in the most unlikely of industry settings, wherever management sees how to give front-line people attractive learning compacts.

Innovation compacts embody repeated innovation and ongoing learning about new business opportunities. As we saw in Chapter 14, companies famous for their internal entrepreneurs and the number of their new products provide an environment that facilitates the discovery of new opportunities, with easy access to the necessary resources, and an incentive system that avoids punishing failure and rewards initiative. But they also co-ordinate their independent-minded entrepreneurs into a corporate learning network. Co-ordinating the activities of internal entrepreneurs used to be a major challenge. However, distributed computing has made this so much easier that some companies have begun to transform themselves into an innovative network. The basic idea has been to create a network of self-forming, self-managing teams, held together by open information on the IT system and compacts that embody the commitments of one part of the organization to the others.

GRANITE ROCK: AN EXAMPLE OF EFFICIENCY COMPACTS

Granite Rock in California, profiled by John Case in *INC.* magazine, has a quarry, mixes paving material in 17 plants, runs a highway paving operation, and sells building supplies. When Bruce Wolpert, the grandson of the founder, took over, he had an MBA plus eight years of experience with Hewlett Packard. Yet he spent time talking to people throughout the company, in the quarry, the plants, on the road, finding out what they liked and disliked about their jobs. He also asked them which companies they admired most because of excellent products and service. At the same time, Wolpert put together his own management team from both inside and outside the company. Together they began putting in the elements of a systematic approach to learning from top to bottom, based on collecting information about what is happening, analyzing what it means, designing a new approach, and moving into action on an individual and team level.

One of the most important jobs of a manager, according to Wolpert, 'is to make sure there's a flood of information coming in to the company'. Granite Rock gets its information from the usual sources; customers, internal operations, and external benchmarking. But Wolpert insists on creativity in finding the information. In addition to annual customer 'report cards' rating Granite against competitors, periodic focus groups looking for new ideas, and longer more detailed surveys every few years, the company hands out 'quick response cards' for comment on products and service delivered today, and provides a 100 per cent service guarantee - no charge for inadequate products or service. Inside the company, managers supplement the usual statistical control charts with data of their choice. In the logistics area, apart from on-time delivery, managers track customer loading time, the number of road service calls, driver attitudes, and so on. Outside, Granite Rock people benchmark competitors, take advantage of supplier seminars and training, and visit other best-in-class companies, like Domino Pizza, for on-time delivery.

Based on the rich supply of information, Wolpert expects the front-line managers and people leading the problem-solving teams to go wherever their solution takes them. The process begins with middle managers, who develop tools for systematic problem solving and assemble multi-functional teams to assess, plan, and implement; for example, a 'product-service discrepancy report' including a 'root-cause analysis' which shows what must be done for the purchase of heavy equipment like bulldozers. (At the time the company was profiled, some 100 teams were in action among the 400 employees.) But the front-line leaders have to ensure thorough execution. Thus, when a team realized that customers often blamed Granite Rock when they ordered the wrong product, or used it incorrectly, they introduced customer training and education, plus a manager measurement reflecting the number of customer seminars they sponsor.

In return for getting information and acting on it, Granite Rock gives its people almost unlimited access to and support for their own training, opportunities for in-house advancement, and high-visibility recognition. In the words of a quarry supervisor: 'I think Bruce wants us all to get a little smarter. We're allowed to learn anything we can'. In addition to in-house courses on problem-solving skills, leadership, and the like, employees can attend customer-run, industry training, and neighbouring college courses, all on company time and expense. Job rotation and internal mobility are hallmarks of the Granite Rock approach. When it comes to hiring, internal candidates get preference. Most of the managers have held positions in several of the divisions. And even hourly employees get training for several jobs.

Instead of relying on job descriptions and performance reviews, everyone maps out a personal accomplishment and development plan, an 'Individual Professional Development Plan' (IPDP), with his or her supervisor once a year. Recognition does not come in the form of equity or large-scale monetary rewards. Rather, every year well over a hundred employees get bonuses of a few hundred to a few thousand dollars for specific achievements. The higher profile reward comes on 'Recognition Day', an annual event at every facility, where the employees entertain top and other unit managers, showing them how much the facility has improved and learned, both individually and collectively, over the past year.

The net result is that Granite Rock has the lowest production costs in its region, with service and quality levels that allow it to charge a 6 per cent price premium, while gaining market share.

The efficiency compact at Granite Rock can be summarized as follows:

Economic dimension

What am I supposed to do?	Problem-solve, execute, follow-through
What help will I get?	Personal training, in-house advancement opportunities
How will I be measured?	Based on Individual Professional Development Plan
What economic reward will I get?	Awards, the chance for job rotation, internal promotion

Social dimension

What vision will I share?	Make Granite Rock the high-quality, low-cost leader
What values will I share?	Common sense, action orientation, mutual help
What informal rules will apply?	Information sharing, systematic problem solving, internal mobility, commitment to personal goals

Psychological dimension

How good is it for me?	Show what I can do, dynamic work environment
How risky is it for me?	Risk I don't meet my development plan
What personal satisfaction will I get?	Personal accomplishment, high-profile recognition

The Individual Personal Development Plan is at the heart of these efficiency-based learning compacts. In effect, the IPDPs are rolling front-line compacts, revised annually during the discussions between supervisors and employees. They are notable because they take learning all the way to the front line in the quarries, trucks, and so on. The ongoing compact renewal builds in the opportunity for progressive learning. As in all learning compacts, the rewards in these efficiency-based learning compacts are mainly on the psychological dimension, in this case, in the form of team accomplishment, personal development, and recognition.

OTICON: AN EXAMPLE OF INNOVATION COMPACTS

Oticon, the Danish hearing aid manufacturer, has received a lot of publicity for its innovation-oriented, networking compacts. Some commentators have held up its so-called 'spaghetti organization' as an example of the elusive, chaotic organization of the future. A more realistic view, however, is that Oticon represents one dimension of what it takes to build a company that can shape its environment. It is a good example of the ongoing innovating arm of a competitive company.

The Oticon story started with the appointment of Lars Kolind as CEO in 1988. The company was losing money, so Kolind's first task was to turn it around. He did it in the standard way: cutting costs and loss-making activities. But there was a feeling that not much fundamental had changed: 'Although I had cut costs and loss-making product lines and activities, I didn't believe that would significantly improve our competitive position in the long term'. On New Year's day 1990, Kolind wrote a four page memo outlining his vision for the future. Kolind asked his people to 'think the unthinkable': all paper, walls, and jobs would go, to be replaced by dialogue and action to get creativity, speed, and productivity. 'We wanted to combine innovation with new records in productivity.'

Kolind then asked his people to examine their jobs and identify what they did well; in effect, to redesign their compacts. He wanted every employee to do several jobs, the one he or she did very well, and other tasks where new skills could be learned to pursue innovation. With multi-skilling, Kolind believed people could better understand the jobs of others, reduce the need for time-wasting controls, and contribute to innovation.

To trigger the transformation, he proposed moving the head office to a remote production site in Jutland. The resistance to this move gradually turned into a revolt. Kolind relented. What he didn't expect, however, was the strong support for an innovation-based organization, unleashed by his change of mind: 'I gave in on where Oticon is going to relocate, but I insisted on carrying through with the reorganization ... From one week to the next there was a complete change'. Kolind called in the media to cover the reorganization, and they came in droves to witness the pre-announced Oticon innovation revolution. But he was not merely after publicity: 'I made no secret of the fact that I was using the press as a tool, as a way of burning the bridges behind us'.

Project leaders, most of whom had innovation compacts, were the centrepiece of the new organization. Project leaders might offer their services to, or be recruited by, the management committee. To assemble their teams, project leaders had access to available employees and resources throughout the company, using the IT system to see who was free, plus persuasion and negotiation to bring them on board. Team members rotated from project to project, working on two or more at the same time. The information system listed current commitments. People soon developed reputations as good or bad colleagues to have on board. As one manager put it: 'In the past, your importance was related to your position, now it comes from your contribution'. Skill co-ordinators maintained basic competencies in each area through personal development reviews, additional training, and recruiting. Bonuses were given mainly for team performance.

After Oticon put the new organization and innovation compacts in place, they introduced two important new products in 18 months, half the time previously required. Moreover, over two years, Oticon quadrupled its profits and increased its previously flat sales by 13 per cent and 23 per cent, respectively.

The innovation compact at Oticon can be summarized as follows:

Economic dimension

What am I supposed to do?
Discover opportunities for innovation

What help will I get?
Sponsorship, access to information and training

How will I be measured?
Team performance, personal development reviews

What economic reward will I get?
Salary increases and team bonuses.

Social dimension

What vision will I share?
Make Oticon the leading niche player in hearing aids

What values will I share?
Openness, low power distance, flexibility, team spirit

What informal rules will apply?
Create one's own job, remove barriers, involve people

Psychological dimension

How good is it for me?
Opportunity to take initiative, develop personally

How risky is it for me?
Innovation risky, but Kolind understands this

What personal satisfaction will I get?
Scope to innovate, lead a highly motivated team

In effect, the project leaders renewed their compacts each time they took on a new project, albeit within the context of the new organization. By the same token, individual employees renewed compacts when they agreed to join a new project team. The continual rotation between projects resulted in an ongoing renewal of compacts, always adapted to the innovation task at hand.

This type of innovation-based learning compact is most attractive on the psychological dimension. By contrast, it offers little in the way of economic reward. The flexibility, freedom and challenge appeal to independent, entrepreneurial types. It is less appropriate for the detailed, problem-solving work required for continual cost reduction and more appropriate in a small high-tech company. Indeed, at Oticon, the spaghetti organization and innovation compacts were limited to the headquarters people in R&D and marketing.

ENABLING PROCESSES FOR LEARNING COMPACTS

The organizational processes for supporting learning compacts have to be installed and maintained. These processes can be broadly categorized as:

- collecting and sharing information
- developing employee learning skills
- developing useful frameworks and routines.

In companies moving towards learning compacts, some combination of managers in information systems, human resources, and finance and control usually carry out these activities.

Collecting and sharing information

To encourage learning-based compacts, a company must have a corporate-wide memory, or database, which incorporates internal information and experience, and external data on and from customers, competitors, and other partners. This database provides the reference against which individuals can measure how much they have learned to make the company more competitive. Modern information technology has greatly facilitated the development and sharing of such corporate-wide memories. Previously, most corporate information was in the form of accounting data, manuals and procedures, and in the heads of people, all of which were difficult to access; now middle managers increasingly have the task of ensuring that a user-friendly IT system captures the relevant data and experience for everyone to access.

195

Databases listing individuals with their skills and experience are increasingly common, which makes it much easier for everyone to take advantage of everyone else's experience. The more successful service and high-tech companies are farthest along in this respect.

Developing employee learning skills

The information is of little use, however, unless people use it to solve problems and improve efficiency on the one hand, and innovate and create opportunities on the other hand. This requires decentralized, diverse, and continual, learning opportunities, such as on-the-job twinning to learn from others, job rotation, and involvement in teams. Most large multinationals have programmes to provide the corresponding skills and foster a learning mindset.

At the Canadian Imperial Bank of Commerce (CIBC), the man in charge of this is Hubert Saint-Onge, Vice-President, Learning Organization and Leadership Development. CIBC has defined the objectives of employee education in terms of 'what people must know to serve customers'. Saint-Onge and his team have developed a series of 'competency models', about 50 in all, which describe the different human talents that CIBC requires, for example, selling skill, credit analysis expertise, and so on. To develop a particular talent, employees can use books and software at their local branch learning room, shadow colleagues to learn from them on the job, or take a course.

The key to the CIBC approach, however, is that employee learning sits in the hands of employees. They are personally responsible for enhancing and adding to their own portfolio of skills. Employees are expected to develop the skills they need for their job, the range and depth required by a vice-president being different from that of a branch manager, or customer service representative. There is no one in Human Resources to tell them what they should take next. The Training Department is gone. In the words of Saint-Onge: 'Most companies can't tell you how much they spend on training. It took us six months to decipher $30 million a year! And one penny out of a hundred hits the mark'. To correct this, CIBC training is now up to the employees, but it should be designed to perform their current job better, not prepare for the next one. Department heads track how fast their people are learning new skills and where they are apparently not doing enough.

The learning compacts at CIBC can be summarized as follows:

Economic dimension

What am I going to do?	Enhance skills, continually change the way I work
What help will I get?	Local learning room, colleagues, courses
How will I be measured?	Competency models completed, competency lacking
What's in it for me economically?	Learning progress. Employability outside

Social dimension

What vision will I share?	Make CIBC number one
What values will I share?	Responsibility for own learning and development
What informal rules will apply?	Mutual commitment to share, learn from one another

Psychological dimension

How good is it for me?	Open-ended way of developing myself
How risky is it for me?	May fall behind everyone else, without realizing it
What personal satisfaction will I get?	Mastering skills, in charge of my own destiny

In contrast to the compacts that emerge from a one-time change process, this one incorporates a commitment to personal learning, in the form of a continual improvement in the way one works through the acquisition of new skills.

Developing useful frameworks and routines

The development and sharing of useful frameworks and routines for innovation and efficiency improvement is essential to support learning compacts. Recognizing this, some pioneering companies have appointed middle managers to identify, measure, and manage the development of such corporate know-how. Thus, Skandia Assurance and Financial Services (Skandia AFS), the rapidly growing savings and investment products division of the Skandia Insurance Company in Sweden, has appointed both a Director and Controller of Intellectual Capital. The task of the first Intellectual Capital Director, Leif Edvinsson, was to identify, package, capitalize on, and further develop 'intangible and non-material items.'

Edvinsson and his team identified five focus areas of intellectual capital (or know-how), that is, areas with distinct frameworks and routines:

- financial performance
- customer-related
- process efficiency
- renewal projects
- human competencies.

For each of these, they put together a set of measures of the quantity and quality of available frameworks and routines. Once the measures had been identified and tried out in pilot form, Skandia AFS appointed an Intellectual Capital Controller to collect the corresponding data across the group. The combination of the five sets of measures was described as 'Skandia's Business Navigator', a metaphor used for both internal and external communication of the state of Skandia's available frameworks and routines.

The next step was moving from measurement to management of know-how. A 1995 meeting of 25 controllers from around the group decided that all business units would begin using the indicators in the 1996 planning and reporting process. There was also discussion about how to set objectives for know-how development and the kind of bonus and incentive scheme that could be linked to it. In addition, the information technology people began establishing an 'international electronic knowledge networking and sharing system' to share knowledge and information with employees. The local area networks were connected into a global area network allowing all subsidiaries to access one another's databases. For example:

- Everyone could access the central libraries of Skandia AFS presentation materials.
- The IT function of smaller offices could be run from larger offices elsewhere.
- Product and fund information was distributed to thousands of brokers to demonstrate product features to customers and print out application forms for them on the spot in the local broker's office.
- The Business Navigator was made available on managers' desktops.
- A data bank was developed on employees with information on their current job, competencies, experience, education, and training.

The employee information bank was important because it permitted employees to develop their own 'Personal Navigator' describing the state of their individual know-how in the same terms as that of the company.

In May 1995, Bjorn Wolrath, the CEO of Skandia group called a 'Corporate Council' meeting for the top 150 managers of the Skandia Group to discuss the next steps, as he put it, moving from 'managing through instructions' to 'managing through values'. In 'Qualification Accounts' employees listed what they had accomplished during the year, projects worked on, development and training completed. These qualification accounts were linked to the Personal Navigators. Other frameworks available for enhancing one's own leadership behaviour included 'work permits', introduced at an earlier 1992 Skandia AFS meeting, a statement expressing the freedom employees had to collaborate, be curious and speak up. Other routines, such as job rotation and projects outside one's unit, were also discussed.

Most importantly, Wolrath closed the Corporate Council meeting by asking those present to send him a letter saying how they would contribute to the Skandia vision, develop the intellectual capital, and the trust needed for that in their business units. He wanted each manager to include in the letter three actions they would personally undertake to build a high trust culture in Skandia. About a month later Wolrath personally responded to each of the letters, outlining what he would do to help. The managers then repeated this process with their people.

The learning compacts at Skandia can be summarized as follows:

Economic dimension

What am I supposed to do?	Improve performance, contribute to intellectual capital
What help will I get?	Frameworks and routines, 'work permits' to learn
How will I be measured?	Business Navigator, plus my Qualification Account
What economic reward will I get?	Bonus, incentives linked to learning and company know-how

Social dimension

What vision will I share?	Exploit intellectual capital for competitive advantage
What values will I share?	Learning and trust needed to create intellectual capital
What informal rules will apply?	Learning objectives, freedom to collaborate, curiosity

Psychological dimension

How good is it for me?	Extensive learning infrastructure linked to compensation
How risky is it for me?	Bottom line may suffer affecting us all
What personal satisfaction will I get?	Control own destiny, contribute to intellectual capital

In effect, with the letters he asked the top 150 to send him, Wolrath got his managers to design and sign learning compacts for themselves and their people. Those involved agreed to the objective on their part of a continually improving, personal qualification account, as well as helping to develop corporate intellectual capital and trust. For its part, the company provided an implicit 'work permit' that gave them the freedom and support to learn. These learning compacts, comprising a Personal Navigator, Qualification Account, and Work Permit, went well beyond those at CIBC by incorporating an explicit commitment to corporate learning, supported by an expanding infrastructure for capturing and sharing both information and know-how in the form of shared frameworks and routines.

The CBIC and Skandia examples show how companies can support learning compacts by helping employees develop the necessary skills, by sharing information, and by making useful frameworks and routines available throughout the company. These supports are essential regardless of whether the learning contracts are efficiency or innovation based. However, if the change is to be ongoing, it is essential that learning compacts extend all the way to the top.

ENABLING BEHAVIOUR FOR LEARNING COMPACTS AT THE TOP

At the head of the organization, there is no one but yourself, to provide the context for your learning. To learn yourself and, in particular, to look ahead for the next change over the horizon, you have to develop three habits:

- humility: sensitivity to meaningful feedback
- honesty: objective self-evaluation
- hunger: psychological drive to succeed.

The difficulty of learning at the top is illustrated by what happened at Oticon, the Danish hearing aid company discussed earlier, after it successfully changed its organization into a new flexible network. The new organization led to the rapid introduction of new products, but it also resulted in losses at first. These losses were compounded by a product launch in the USA which failed completely. Yet Lars Kolind, the CEO, had difficulty updating his own compact to focus on cost control. As Kolind recalls, 'Having just loosened everything a lot, it was difficult to tighten up again'.

Without the necessary perspective, it is only natural to blame negative feedback on others. Even Jack Welch of GE fame fell into this trap. As GE's financial progress started to slow down in the mid-eighties, and some big automation investments went bad, Welch tried to find out why. When he started getting the same questions over and over at the GE Management Centre, he couldn't believe it: 'This is unbelievable! I'm getting the same questions I've gotten for five years! Doesn't anybody understand anything? I'm just not getting through to them'. At this point, you need a call for humility, from inside or outside yourself.

Humility: sensitivity to meaningful feedback

To move towards learning and the continual renewal of your own compact, you must be sensitive to negative, but potentially meaningful, feedback. The challenge in adopting a learning compact at the top is that compact renewal has to be largely self-driven, with little facilitation from anyone else, apart from close members of the management team, or the board. At Oticon, Kolind had a board that sensed there was not enough control and pushed him to appoint a financial director. Kolind listened and, in early 1992, Niels Jacobsen arrived as Executive Vice-President of Oticon.

At GE, Welch got help from Jim Baughmann, GE's head of management development, who played a big role in proposing and setting up the Workouts. In the firing line of the first Workouts, Welch got direct feedback from junior colleagues, not only about how GE was doing, but also, indirectly, about how he was doing. He began to realize that his commander style was no longer working. People were exhausted and demoralized. Something new was needed. Part of the problem was Jack Welch himself. The old social compact Welch had with his people for the purposes of the turnaround had unravelled. People were no longer willing to play by the same informal rules of the game that had developed for the turnaround. They were unwilling to talk about empowerment and accept top-down directives.

Honesty: objective self-evaluation

You have to be honest with yourself about what feedback on your behaviour and business performance means. The question is whether you can deploy the same leadership style for the next change effort. Can a radical cost-cutter, for example, also inspire entrepreneurship? Would you want to? Do you have what it takes in new skills and energy to lead more change? To answer these questions, you need a good dose of honesty and self-knowledge.

At Oticon, Kolind saw his limitations. Instead of trying to manage control, he let Jacobsen do it. While Kolind took responsibility for R&D, Sales and Marketing, and overall strategy, Jacobsen focused on day-to-day operational issues. 'He was a great help in managing the business more effectively, but it was not easy ... He was constantly reminding us about the bottom line ... He had the determination and motivation to put everything together.' The arrival of Jacobsen brought people into the organization whose main compact orientation was problem-solving cost control. By constantly 'reminding everyone about the bottom line', Jacobsen pushed everyone else to revise their economic compacts to include a concern for costs. As a result, profits began to recover strongly and, in a very flat market, sales started going up by double digit percentages.

At GE, it was not too difficult for Welch to figure out that, if he wanted to keep the company on its earnings growth path, he had to unleash the talent of his people. The question is how he convinced himself that he could change his compact with his people. How could he shift from being the commander – he'd been called 'Neutron Jack' during the turnaround – to being an inspirational leader capable of unleashing the potential of his people? Although he obviously had an ego commensurate with the job and was known to be very competitive, he was also credited with being honest with himself. In the words of one board member at the time he was appointed CEO, 'He wanted you to know who he was. That was a very appealing quality for leadership. To be self-confident, to be honest with yourself'.

Hunger: the psychological drive to succeed

Welch had one other quality that is central to revising one's own compact spontaneously. He had an insatiable appetite to grow personally. Welch knew he had to make some important changes to his leadership compact if the empowerment thing was to fly. He called for:

> 'redefining the relationship between boss and subordinate ... In the new culture, the role of the leader is to express a vision, get buy-in, and implement it. That calls for open caring relationships with every employee, and face-to-face communication.'

According to then GE vice-president, Larry Bossidy: ' He's a man obsessed with growth, personal growth. If you came back and interviewed him a year from now, he won't be the same guy you interviewed today'.

To what extent did Welch really change his own behaviour? According to Larry Bossidy, who had known Welch for a long time, quite a bit:

'I do think there was change, vividly, from yelling and screaming for performance, to a much more motivational kind of approach. He became a lot more understanding, much more tolerant. Hey, if you get the job done even though your style is different from mine, that's fine. He wasn't that way in the beginning.'

On the other hand, casual comments from GE managers reveal that fear is still an important part of Welch's style. At GE management meetings, Welch talks about how he had to 'take out' various managers for not meeting their targets, or not living up to GE's espoused values. Nobody knows whether Welsh's drive to succeed got the better of his self-honesty when he decided to try and change his style.

The Oticon example, on the other hand, illustrates a learning compact at the top based not on trying to change oneself, but on changing the composition of the top team to reflect the shifting forces of change. Whereas front-line people can concentrate on a particular type of focused learning that suites their style, learning at the top either means adopting a management style that is not the manager's natural one, as in the case of Welch, or maintaining one's style and changing the team to deal with the shifting needs of the whole organization, as in Kolind's case. Neither approach is possible without a strong drive to succeed, to beat the odds against surviving major change at the top.

Whatever approach you take to developing your own learning compacts, the key is an ongoing willingness to learn. This is vital, if you are to nurture learning compacts on the front line, and orchestrate shifts in those compacts, so your company can both adapt to the business environment and shape it as described in Chapter 16.

REORIENTING LEARNING
COMPACTS TO OUTPACE
THE COMPETITION

HEWLETT PACKARD: REORIENTING LEARNING

Lew Platt, the CEO of Hewlett Packard, urges his managers to be 'always looking over your shoulder at the competition, always thinking about the next move', He talks about learning flexibility as a critical part of 'healthy paranoia'. To maintain competitive advantage, he nurtures the HP practice of bringing new technology to market, even if it risks cannibalizing the sales of existing products:

> 'Withholding technology or the next price cut may seem like a good way to maximize profit margins, but it's a deadly game … Whatever we're doing that made us successful today won't be good tomorrow, I can guarantee that.'

HP's ability to reorient the emphasis of its divisional managers' efforts rapidly and repeatedly, between innovation-oriented and efficiency-oriented learning, has allowed it to outpace the competition in some of the world's most rapidly evolving markets. In 1993, products developed in the previous two years accounted for two-thirds of the company's sales. By 1994, HP had become the second largest US computer company, being the world leader in 'open system' minicomputers, printers, test and measurement equipment, second in workstations, and eighth, rising rapidly, in PCs. It was among the top six PC-makers by 1995, and poised to move to one of the top three by 1997.

To outpace the competition, you have to master the two skills that are key to reorienting front-line learning compacts:

- getting the direction right at the top; and
- signalling the need for a reorientation of compacts.

GETTING THE DIRECTION RIGHT AT THE TOP

HP has been able to shift the compact emphasis of its people from innovation to efficiency, and back to innovation, in order to exploit successive industry shifts. The only significant organizational error it seems to have made was to shift too far in the direction of marketing centralization in the mid-eighties. How was it able to get the direction right so many times?

To get the direction right, the leadership compact must include the following features:

- clarity about the company's distinctive competencies
- learning from stakeholder feedback
- openness to continual experimentation
- periodic fresh thinking in top management.

At HP, the leadership compact is based on a very clear, open view of the company's value-creating strengths on the economic dimension and the 'HP Way of Doing Business' on the social dimension. HP emphasizes its product development programmes: the R&D budget hovers around 10 per cent of sales; expansion into new markets only goes ahead with innovative new product ideas. HP also has an outstanding sales and support organization, providing consulting, training, hardware and software, to ensure superior customer satisfaction; no products are marketed before being thoroughly tested and specified. These distinctive competencies determine HP's long-run direction. Together with substantial experience in providing computer systems for both the technical and business markets, these strengths led HP's management to put together a computer strategy in the early eighties around four basic points. First, they knew that customer satisfaction depended on user-friendly customized software open to all kinds of information, and integrated networks compatible with all kinds of software. They also knew that their best way of getting there was to bring to bear the power of HP product innovation. What they didn't know was how best to organize the learning effort.

Second, the leadership compact at HP includes learning from the feedback of its stakeholders, customers, suppliers, employees, and third, an openness to continual experimentation with new product/market directions. HP realigns its network of product divisions so often that when a particular shift doesn't work, there is little psychological or political resistance to shifting it again to find the right direction. HP tried a more centralized approach for its computer marketing in the mid-eighties, but quickly accepted that it wasn't working in the marketplace. In fact, efficiency and cost reduction were needed to deal with the downturn. Although cost reduction of the intensity practised at the turn of the decade had not been part of the normal HP flexibility, the ability to tack quickly in different directions in pursuit of the longer-term strategic objective brought the need for efficiency into management's sights more quickly. Once it had restructured to lower costs, HP had relatively little difficulty tacking back in the direction of more innovation to attack the home market.

Fourth, the leadership compacts at the top include a readiness to bring new thinking into top management by promoting strong people. At HP, in the mid-eighties, it was Dean Morton, the newly promoted Chief Operating Officer, who helped shift the priority to cost leadership. In 1992, when Young and Morton retired after more than 30 years at HP, the new CEO, Lew Platt initiated the drive back to more innovation.

SIGNALLING THE NEED FOR A REORIENTATION OF LEARNING COMPACTS

The challenge is to orchestrate a shift in the overall emphasis of compact renewal to support the right direction for value creation. Although both innovation and efficiency-based learning are needed at all times, the required emphasis varies with shifts in the value-creating opportunities in the marketplace. To get the shift in emphasis, you need cues to signal the new preferred direction for learning compacts as shown in Figure 16.1.

New Direction	Cues
Innovation	Reorganization around new *separate* product/market segments, new channels, development alliances, with new measurement and reward systems
Efficiency	Set up new groups, alliances, process teams, and/or other forms of internal, or external *co-operation*, as well as new measurement and reward systems

Figure 16.1 Cues for reorienting learning compacts

These cues presume that learning compacts are already in place; in other words, people are already continually renewing their compacts with a view to changing what they do or how they do things. Since their compact renewal is self-driven, all they need to modify their learning direction is a signal about the new direction for value creation and an enabling process. If learning compacts are not in place, then standard compact renewal, as described in Part II, is needed.

REORIENTATION OF LEARNING COMPACTS AT HEWLETT PACKARD

HP has the basics in place: employees with experience driving change, supported by a social compact, and enabling processes, that encourage ongoing learning and initiative on the front line.

Lew Platt, CEO since 1992, says:

'Senior management's role is not to tell business units what opportunity to take. Instead, our role is to create the environment that encourages business managers to take risks and create new growth opportunities. In other words, vision at HP isn't a strait-jacket that constrains our managers, but rather a view of the many opportunities ahead.'

Platt encourages and supports risk-taking:

> 'He is very supportive of people who try something that doesn't work out. He is almost protective of people who stick their necks out.'

And perhaps most important, according to one of his general managers:

> 'He is in touch. He knows what's going on in the organization. And he makes sure everyone knows what they are doing is important ... Lew is not impressed with himself ... He hasn't lost sight of the fact that we are successful because of the people.'

The whole company is held together by an unusually powerful social compact, enshrined in the famous 'HP Way', the company's set of corporate objectives and values. 'Informality, trust, and respect for individual initiative were the norms, along with a commitment to teamwork and participative decision-making', with promotion from within and job rotation across functional areas.

HP's flexibility had its origins in innovation-based learning compacts on the front line. The firm grew up with electronic test and measurement instruments for scientists and engineers. The company took pride in the high percentage of its sales that came from new products introduced over the previous three years. Backed up by superior technology, HP could sell these essentially stand-alone products at a premium price to technical customers who needed little service. Since the market segments were well defined, the products were naturally grouped into independent product lines, produced and marketed by independent product divisions. The divisions acted as tactical business units with considerable freedom to manage R&D, manufacturing, marketing, finance, and personnel. Divisions were never allowed to grow to more than about a thousand people, before being split into new smaller divisions. This system nurtured front-line managers with innovation-based learning compacts, who were strongly entrepreneurial.

Reorganizing around new product/market segments for innovation

To provide a focus for innovation, HP organized the divisions into product groups, with the sales organizations managed at the group level, separately from the product divisions. Strategy was also developed at the group level in line with the corporate vision and values, and cascaded down to the divisions in the form of short-range and long-range divisional objectives, set in co-operation with the divisional managers. The divisions had great freedom of implementation.

As the markets have evolved, so the cues have shifted back and forth between innovation and efficiency. The basic approach has been to use organizational cues and rely on the flexibility of the individual learning compacts for adaptation to the new direction. With product divisions as the basic building blocks, the company could adapt to the evolving business environment and the need for innovation by redrawing the product group boundaries. This reoriented the innovation compacts of the divisional managers. A key issue in the reorganizations was the regrouping of the sales organizations. The first product groups came into being in 1969, with the establishment of a Data Products Group for computers and an Electronic Products Group for instrumentation. After rapid growth, in a second major regrouping in 1974, HP created six product groups. And in 1979, the computer side of the business was reorganized into five groups. Overall, in 1982, there were 12 product groups covering 45 divisions. Computer product sales grew from 16.8 per cent in 1971 to 51 per cent of total sales in 1982 and HP was the seventh largest computer manufacturer in the world.

New co-ordinating activities for efficiency

In contrast to the instrument markets, the computer market did not have well-defined segments, customers wanted ready-to-use products designed for specific applications reflecting their needs, and competition was fierce. To cope with these market requirements, the compacts of the divisional managers were reoriented towards more co-operation, by introducing cross-divisional co-ordinating activities.

First, the company set up a 'Computer Strategy Council' with the top management from the information processing divisions. Among other things, the council sponsored an applications-oriented marketing strategy, which combined planning and control applications, factory automation, office systems, and engineering, for customers in manufacturing industries. New divisions started developing software for this and other markets. Among the start-ups was an Applications Marketing Division to provide sales support in delivering the software to customers.

HP also formed other lower level committees, or councils, as ongoing teams to deal with cross-functional issues, such as the co-ordination of fabrication shop activities. Short-term task forces of five to ten people from different functions were put together to deal with specific micro issues, like a conference for training sales people. The corresponding compacts for these councils and committees resembled those of sponsoring and co-ordinating change teams with an emphasis on process management.

Newly appointed programme managers gave unified direction to cross-divisional projects. They had the authority to use whatever resources the project needed from the divisions involved, to develop and market new products. These managers also had process responsibilities. HP's first 32-bit computer system was developed in this way, by a programme manager with a project team, from the combined inputs of ten different product divisions. Taken together, the roles of the programme managers, councils, and committees, balanced the traditional HP innovation compacts with a mix of efficiency-oriented, problem-solving compacts.

Centralization for even more efficiency

Yet, some people believed that the managerial compacts needed even more of an emphasis on co-ordination. One expert suggested that HP was 'a classic case of the engineering-driven company confronting a marketing-driven world and that they should restructure to acknowledge that'. In 1983, HP announced a reorganization of its computer business to 'provide improved strategic focus' and 'strengthen channels of customer interaction'. The new structure created groups for larger workstations and operating software, for terminals and personal computers, for peripherals, printers and data communication. The big change, however, was that all computer marketing was centralized in the Computer Marketing Group, and all development of integrated solutions moved under the umbrella of the Business Development Group.

The new organization tilted many learning compacts away from innovative entrepreneurship towards a larger integrated team effort. According to a Business Development Group manager: 'Division managers who have a marketing orientation will be most resistant. They'll feel like they're losing something, such as the fun of creative marketing.' Even though the new structure took marketing freedom away from the product divisions, in true HP style most people rallied to the new organization. As an operations manager put it:

> 'There is tremendous trust and faith in management's actions. We know there are enough bright people around who will say something before a decision is final ... This checks-and-balances system works because there is trust and open communication.'

Nevertheless, some managers were not convinced. One division general manager said:

> 'I think we will pay the price of over-staffing during the transition period ... We can't afford to drop any balls. This is especially true as we consolidate sales development teams from divisions into the centralized sales centres.'

The new organization delivered very uneven results. The group concentrating on high-end workstations and related products went from strength to strength. It embodied HP's core engineering skills. HP's

216

workstations and 'open system' servers for computer networks became a leading choice for those moving away from mainframes. The group responsible for peripherals and printers, starting with an early lead in the business printer market, also did well. In 1988, it made a breakthrough, introducing the first high quality inkjet printer which displaced the Japanese mechanical 'dot matrix' printers. But the Personal Computer Group had problems. In the eyes of the market, the company's PCs remained boring and overpriced.

Reorganization again around product/market segments to find the right innovation focus

The premium placed on marketing co-operation in the 1983 reorganization seemed to have undermined the innovation side of the PC managers' compacts. Product managers didn't have the same feel for the market and so they could not shape it. The PC market was quite volatile in terms of customer and consumer preferences. A key problem was the over-centralized approach to marketing: HP's centralized marketing and sales had difficulty getting timely information back to the product divisions. To deal with these problems, HP reversed the centralized approach to marketing and regrouped its PC product divisions several times in search of an appropriate innovation focus, before it was overtaken by recession.

New structure and systems again for efficiency

When the PC market went into recession in the late eighties, HP's high cost base made it difficult to compete. Containing costs is one of the most difficult challenges for companies with a learning bias towards entrepreneurship and innovation. However, the threat of red ink helps to focus the mind. During the recession in the late 1980s and early 1990s, computer prices fell and gross margins declined across the industry. HP cut its workforce and eliminated bureaucracy, as it shifted priorities towards achieving a 'leadership cost structure' in each business. HP cut its operating expenses from more than 40 per cent of revenues in 1988 to 28 per cent in the first quarter of 1994. Between 1989 and 1994, the number of employees remained constant at 98 000, while sales doubled from $12 billion to $25 billion. In 1992, the company restructured its PC business, closing 10 out of the 12 factories. 'You make investments and take your losses for a period, but then you have to test the viability of a business by its profitability', says Bob Wyman, chief financial officer, 'Each business has to stand on its own, be profitable and finance its own growth'. To improve their efficiency further, each of the businesses was encouraged to move from a functional to a process organization. This emphasis on continually improving efficiency and productivity laid the basis for HP's next move in the PC market.

Reorganizing again around product/market alliances for a renewed innovation focus

In October 1994, HP decided it wanted to get in on the boom for home PCs with multimedia and all sorts of peripherals, such as cable modems and scanners, set-top TV boxes and home PC networks. The idea was to capitalize on its brand name and distribution network for printers, while copying the lean, outsourcing approach of successful competitors. In November, the company created its Home Products Division and had products in stores for sales trials by March 1995. It outsourced motherboards, assembly, and calls to its 0800 number service lines. In April, less than six months after the Home Products Division was formed, HP launched a line of low-priced multimedia PCs through Circuit City, a major retail chain with more than 300 stores. To establish itself in the market, HP doubled the number of chains carrying its home products and cut prices three times in six months.

None of this flexibility and rapid action would have been possible without a return to innovation learning compacts, based on fiercely independent, decentralized product divisions, with large autonomy in calling marketing shots. 'HP's at a crossroads. We're looking at mass markets, consumer markets, digital imaging, whole new channels of distribution', according to Roger Wilson, director of corporate communications in Europe. Managing innovation-based learning compacts with an external network of retailers and suppliers is part of this new era at HP.

Signs of a shift back again to co-ordination for efficiency

Not surprisingly, the first signs of the next shift in direction and reorientation of compacts are already in sight. 'Cross-organizational collaboration' is coming back into vogue at HP to co-ordinate the drive for larger markets. A new council of top technical and marketing staff throughout the company has taken on the task of identifying new 'multi-disciplinary' products. In the words of Joel Birnbaum, head of HP's research labs, 'We're hunting for big game.'

OUTPACING THE COMPETITION

The HP story, especially in the PC industry, shows how a company can come from behind and outpace the competition, by using organizational cues to reorient front-line learning compacts. But it hasn't always been easy.

Following HP's moves in the PC market, one can see the difficulty the company had penetrating the market in the mid-eighties when it was invaded by the large-scale arrival of clones from South East Asia. HP soon discovered that its PCs were not innovative enough and too expensive to make a dent in the market. HP made little real progress, until its first breakthrough came, not from a top-down move, but from learning on the front line. It was the development of the high quality ink-jet printer that generated a real HP presence in the PC-peripherals market. The second big move started with the decision at the top to become a low cost leader in the late eighties. This eventually put HP in the position to challenge the market leaders with successive price cuts. HP's third big move emerged in the mid-nineties out of front-line exploration of the possibilities in the home and multimedia market, encouraged from the top, first, by co-ordinating mechanisms across the product divisions concerned, and then, with focus to create the Home Products Division.

In addition to the importance of compact reorientation from the top, the HP story illustrates how heavily outpacing depends on the flexibility of individual learning compacts. The HP front-line tradition of spontaneous entrepreneurship has continually generated crucial innovations. The flexibility of the product divisions has continually provided the base for new product combinations to attack emerging market segments. In brief, it is the timely combination of top-down reorientation with ongoing compact renewal, that allows a company to take charge of its industry. Outpacing demands new compacts for change.

LOOKING INTO THE FUTURE

What happens to compacts as the pace of business keeps accelerating with more and more being done in a shifting, electronic web of virtual relationships? What are the implications for compact design and renewal?

The signs are that explicit compacts are even more important, because less and less can be taken for granted in the evolving relationship between an individual and an organization. The principles of compact design and renewal described in the preceding chapters require special attention. In addition, there is an extra need for flexibility and ongoing, self-driven compact renewal. We can summarize the compact design and renewal principles, with reference to the emerging, interconnected economy, as follows.

START WITH TODAY'S REALITY

The people in every organization, whether of the traditional, or the virtual kind, have compacts that reflect the reality they experience. Since people remain people, their responses to a change initiative will continue to fall at least into the four clusters of change agents, bystanders, traditionalists, and resistors. To commit to a new change initiative, each cluster needs a bridge between their existing compacts and new ones.

What is different from the past, for more and more organizations, is that the new reality involves increasing speed with shorter and shorter cycle times of all types and more rapid obsolescence of assets, processes, products, and know-how. One of the key success factors is the rate of learning. As the Hewlett-Packard story in the previous chapter shows, those who can learn more rapidly ride ahead of the wave.

The second new reality is the spreading network, or web of project-based relationships, both within companies and with independent outsiders. For example, in Southern California's entertainment and new media industry, tens of thousands of new jobs have been created since the mid-nineties, not by giant studios, but in a loose network of independent producers, writers, directors, artists, and technical people. People assemble around projects and when they're over reassemble around new ones, taking their talents with them.

The third new reality is that more and more employees are becoming in fact, if not legally, one-person-firms. Flexibility and career independence are the hallmarks of their organizational relationships. As Andy Grove, the founder and retired CEO of Intel, put it:

> 'No matter where you work you are not an employee. You are in business with one employer – yourself – in competition with millions of businesses worldwide … Nobody owes you a career – you own it as a sole proprietor. And the key to survival is to learn to add more value everyday.'

DESIGN COMPACTS WITH AN EYE ON OUTPACING

Regardless of the particular reality that your company faces today, you should design new compacts with an eye on becoming a fast-moving, flexible organization that can outpace the competition. Speed and flexibility are enhanced by getting rid of all unnecessary intermediaries. The previous chapters described the learning compacts, organizational infrastructure, and leadership involved. In brief, the compact frameworks for front-line, middle, and top management in an outpacing organization are:

- *Front-line:*
  - network and discover new opportunities
  - innovation and efficiency-based learning compacts.
- *Middle*
  - select and develop new opportunities
  - manage knowledge development and sharing
  - learning facilitation compacts.
- *Top*
  - develop social compact
  - time full-scale exploitation of opportunities

– reorient front-line compacts
– open to learning at the top.

BUILD A PROCESS BRIDGE FOR COMPACT RENEWAL

The compact renewal context is continually evolving with shifts in the business environment and the varying readiness of your people to commit to yet another change. Don't try to jump into final compacts (unless you intend to work with new people). Build a process bridge. Select a sequence and mix of the basic change processes (top-down turnaround, taskforce change, widespread participation, and bottom-up initiatives) that is both consistent with the starting reality in terms of pressure for, and resistance to, change, and that aims at reinforcing ongoing, bottom-up compact renewal. In a rapidly moving environment, you also need to know quickly who is on board. This requires attention to the opportunities you provide for people to signal their commitment to compact renewal explicitly.

INSPIRE ONGOING COMPACT RENEWAL WITH MEANING

The more your organization moves to bottom-up, self-driven compact renewal, the more important market conditions become in shaping the details on the economic dimension, and the more attention you want to give to the social and psychological aspects.

Economic dimension

In a network, project-based organization, the economic details of compacts are determined by the conditions of supply and demand in the marketplace, whether this is inside, or across the boundaries of the firm. Those individuals whose talents are in excess supply are driven by the economic need to find work. However, those in demand not only want top dollar compensation with option/equity participation, but also look for more on the social and psychological dimensions. This is especially true for the core people with longer-term compacts in key positions.

Social dimension

The more time core people have to spend in front of a screen tending their virtual relationships, the more they look for a social dimension to their compacts which connects them with others directly in a traditional human way. Therefore, the kind of team they're in, as well as the informal rules of behaviour and risk sharing, take on greater significance in shaping their commitment.

Psychological dimension

When they can afford to, independent people emphasize psychological satisfaction, a compact they feel really good about both economically and emotionally. To inspire ongoing compact renewal and retain their commitment, an open-ended framework for value creation, even when it is supported by a strong social compact, may not be enough. More and more successful people are asking what meaning is associated with their value creation. As a result, the ability to develop a compact framework with a larger purpose, with a pioneering role, with an exciting shared vision, will play an increasingly pivotal role in sustaining compact renewal.

APPENDIX 1

How national culture affects compact design and renewal

National culture exerts a subliminal, but nevertheless real, influence on both the content of compact design and the form of its renewal. National culture reflects the values and habits people share, embedded in educational, political, religious, economic, and legal systems.

IMPACT OF CULTURE ON COMPACT DESIGN

The way in which national culture affects compact design can be summarized in terms of the impact of value preferences on the compact dimensions.

Economic dimension

What am I supposed to do?:   Analysis vs. Intuition

The way a company designs new assignments depends on how it thinks and plans. The approach has a lot to do with how intuitive, as opposed to analytical, people are in their decision making. More intuitive companies de-emphasize the formal decision-making routines and strategic planning systems found in analytically-oriented firms; they rely more on common sense in decision making and experience in developing strategy. In the latter case, what people are supposed to do to support change is based on a common sense linkage between the overall value-creating idea and individual assignments, rather than on a detailed planning system. For example, a strong tradition of data collection and analysis and preference for a more analytical approach permeates the design of new economic compacts in many American companies (compared to companies in many other cultures). The widespread use of highly quantitative performance agreements demonstrates this preference.

What help will I get?:   Group vs. Individual

The nature of the help that people get is influenced by how much emphasis is placed on group and team work, as opposed to individual effort. The contrast between the USA and Japan in terms of individual, as opposed to group, orientation has been widely commented upon, with the Japanese being a stark contrast to Americans for their emphasis on group work and harmony, to the point where they seem to lack individual identity. Conversely, the Americans provide a stark contrast to the Japanese in their emphasis on individuality, to the point where they seem indifferent to the impact of their actions on the group, or society. As a result, much greater expectations of help from other members of the larger group are built into compacts in Japan, than in the USA.

How will I be measured?:   Merit vs. Position

The performance assessment built into a compact is influenced by what counts in a culture: is it merit, or position, what you know and do, or who you know? With a long national tradition of linking reward to performance, US companies in general have gone furthest in building that linkage into their internal values and rules, and their compacts. This is supported by concrete data collection and analysis, with quantitative milestones and measures of performance that allow for an appreciation of merit. By contrast, in Japan and Europe, position and reputation can still play an important role in how people are assessed.

What's in it for me?:   Money vs. Intangibles

Money or intangibles: what is the anticipated reward in my compact? While money is important in all cultures that are linked to a market economy, the emphasis varies. In Anglo-Saxon investment banking, for example, money is everything as far as rewards go. In Japanese or Northern European manufacturing, by contrast, recognition and other intangibles play a significant role in the rewards that people look for.

Social dimension

National culture is especially influential on the social dimension, concerned as it is with shared values and the informal rules of the game.

What values and informal rules will apply?:

High vs. Low Power Distance

A high power distance between management and employees, that is, the extent to which hierarchy is important in interpersonal relations, creates ritualized social rules between managers and their people. While such rules are common in all societies, among the leading countries, the Japanese are best known for the implicit structure of their professional relationships. These rules of behaviour are so well ingrained that they take the place of more formal rules, allowing the Japanese to put together compacts with minimal formality on the economic dimension, supported instead by a strong social dimension. Similarly, in Europe, the more one moves to the south, the more elaborate are the social hierarchies and the more implicit the compacts.

Confrontation vs. Compromise

The way disputes are resolved, either through confrontation or compromise, also shapes the way new compacts are designed. The American tradition is for each side to confront the other with a somewhat exaggerated view of the strength of their position and then to probe and, where possible, undercut the other side's strength, before finally negotiating an agreement. The Northern European approach is for both sides to present their view of a balanced assessment of the situation and then criticize the lack of balance on the other side, before finally coming to a compromise. As a result, in many US companies, compacts are often renewed in a unilateral way, with either management dictating most of the terms on a take-it-or-leave-it basis, or on the other extreme, employees having the freedom to design most of the terms their way. By contrast, in Northern Europe, the tradition of negotiated compromise favours a more participative approach to the redesign of compacts. But when the underlying balance of power between management and employees shifts with the economic cycle, compact renewal often gets blocked because neither side is willing to give the other more say in compact design.

Direct vs. Indirect Communication

Some societies, such as the English and the Japanese, are much more indirect than others in the way people communicate what they are thinking and feeling. Indeed, both the English and the Japanese are notorious for often saying the opposite of what they are actually thinking, in order to avoid as much surface unpleasantness in personal interactions as possible. This results is compacts that are heavily driven by the shared implicit rules of the game, in which the form of the relationship can sometimes take precedence over the economic content of the compact.

Emotion vs. Formality

The different cultural preferences for showing what one is feeling, emotion vs. formality, in interpersonal relationships, are illustrated by the contrast between Southern and Northern European cultures. The much greater acceptance of emotional communication in the South brings the psychological dimension of compact design and renewal further into the open, thus favouring new compacts in which each side takes more account of the feelings on the other side, sometimes at the expense of the economic dimension. In the North, the biases are reversed, with people having much greater difficulty discussing the emotional side of a compact, which is often ignored, and thereby results in new compacts that put much greater emotional pressure on both managers and their people.

Psychological dimension

Although what turns people on is very much an individual thing, the classic psychological motivations, such as risk, security, power, and participation are not valued the same way in different cultures.

How risky is it for me?:   Risk vs. Security

In Northern European cultures, security and the preservation of benefits have become a leading objective for large groups of workers faced with the effects of globalization. By contrast, the opportunity to take some risk and shape one's own destiny is more widely appreciated in Anglo-Saxon cultures.

What personal satisfaction will I get?:   Power vs. Participation

Participation is widely appreciated in Northern Europe, to wit the role of labour (albeit contested) on boards and works councils in several countries, whereas power, even if the latest fashion is to play it down, plays a relatively more important role in the compacts of Anglo-Saxon and Southern European managers.

IMPACT OF CULTURE ON THE FORM OF COMPACT RENEWAL

The form of the commitment, the use of written, as opposed to oral buy-in, is affected by common national practice. Oral commitments are more common in cultures with strong unwritten rules of the game, where everybody understands the implications of such commitments and the informal sanctions that will apply if the commitments are not honoured. Thus, compacts in Japan rely more on trust and a sense of mutual obligation between management and the employees. Indeed, it may be taken as an affront if a compact is laid out too explicitly, a sign that one party does not have sufficient confidence that the other knows how things work. Yet, as they grapple with major change, the Japanese are discovering that, even in a homogenous society, commitment can be left too implicit, resulting in a huge waste of time as the parties discover they had different interpretations of what was intended

By contrast, in heterogeneous societies with an Anglo-Saxon common law system of case precedent, there is a strong tradition of very detailed explicit contracts in the legal system. This translates into a preference for more explicit rules in the economic compact with less reliance on the informal rules of the social compact. This preference has been accentuated by the decline in job security and the corresponding rise in the importance of employability, which has made employees much more insistent on spelling out the terms of the compact and relying less on implicit understanding. As a result, even value statements are frequently laid out in explicit terms.

To deal with the impact of culture on compact renewal, you should follow two overall guidelines:

- The bigger the change in national shared values and habits that your new compact framework requires, the more time and effort you have to invest in the compact renewal process to ensure buy-in and follow through.
- The more heterogeneous the culture, the greater the need for written buy-in. Less can be assumed, because people have less in common culturally and, therefore, the more you have to lay things out explicitly.

APPENDIX 2
Bibliographical notes and references

INTRODUCTION

The impact of restructuring on trust, morale, and the relationship with employees, has been receiving increasing attention in business reports. See, for example, the *HR Executive Review: Implementing the New Employment Compact.* (1997) Conference Board, Vol. 4, No. 4, New York and the *International Survey Research: Transition and Transformation: Employee Satisfaction in the '90s (UK).* (1997) International Survey Research Corporation, London.

The concept of a psychological contract originated with Chris Argyris (1957), *Personality and Organization.* Harper and Row, New York and Harry Levinson, (1965) Reciprocation: The Relationship Between Man and Organization, *Administrative Sciences Quarterly.* 9, 370–90, further developed by Edgar H. Schein (1978), *Matching Individual and Organizational Needs.* Addison Wesley, Reading MA.

The compact dimensions overlap somewhat with the three types of commitment, instrumental, moral, and affective, described by Rosabeth Moss Kanter (1972) in *Community and Commitment: Communes and Utopias in Sociological Perspective.* Harvard University Press, June. Note, however, that moral commitment in the form of duty and loyalty to the company itself is becoming less relevant in the face of disappearing job security.

For approaches to contracts in change management, see Sue Dopson and Jean Neumann (1994), 'Uncertainty, Contrariness and the Double-Bind: Middle Managers' Reactions to their Changing Contracts', *Management Research Papers Templeton College*, Oxford, MRP 94/7, April; Denise M. Rousseau (1994), 'Two Ways to Change (and Keep) The Psychological Contract: Theory Meets Practice', *International Consortium for Executive Development Research*, IMD Meeting, April and 'Changing the deal while keeping the people,' *Academy of Management Executive*

(1996), 10, 50–8; also, René Schalk and Charissa Freese (1997), 'New Facets of Commitment in Response to Organizational Change: Research Trends and the Dutch Experience,' *Trends in Organizational Behavior*. 4, 107–23. For some evidence of the critical role of individual task alignment in change management, see Gary Saunders (1996), 'What is the Role of Corporate Vision in Making Change Happen?', *Focus On Change Management*, November 14–18.

For my first steps, see Paul Strebel (1993), 'New Contracts: The Key to Change,' *European Management Journal*, 11, 397–402 and Paul Strebel (1996), 'Why do Employees Resist Change?', *Harvard Business Review*, May/June 86–92.

PART I

Chapter 1

The clustering scheme for change response types was influenced by the 'change arena' in my book Paul Strebel (1992), *Breakpoints: How managers exploit radical business change*. Harvard Business School Press, as well as a framework used in the classroom at IMD by my colleague, Jan Kubes, based in turn on an approach used by Jean-Marie Descarpentries when he was CEO of Glaverbel, at the time part of BSN. For the first presentation of this scheme, see Paul Strebel, (1997) 'The Politics of Change', *IMD Perspectives for Managers*, 2, February. For a different approach taken from the diffusion of innovation, see Sandra Vandermerwe (1995), 'The Process of Market-Driven Transformation', *European Management Journal*, 28, No 2, 79–91.

The stereotypical behaviour patterns of the change response types described in the chapter reflect a range of possible psychological motivations, from power and self-defence on the part of resistors, to security and loyalty on the part of traditionalists, identification and involvement on the part of bystanders, and challenge and self-realization on the part of change agents. While one can imagine other combinations of reaction and motivation, this set covers the terrain most change leaders face. For the underlying psychology, see A. Maslow (1954), *Motivation and Per-*

sonality. New York: Harper & Row; also A. Maslow (1943) 'A Theory of Human Motivation', *Psychological Review*, July 370–96; V. Vroom (1964), *Work and Motivation*. New York: John Wiley & Sons.

The Global Associates story is a disguised case of change in an international financial services firm, based on the author's consulting experience.

Chapter 2

Apart from the company's annual reports, the Eisai story draws heavily on the PhD thesis by Liisa Valikangas, 'Leading a Strategic Transformation at the Top', *Acta Universitatis Tamperensis*. Ser. A Vol. 433, 1994, Appendix C.

The approaches to dealing with the various players, in this and the subsequent chapters, are distilled from innumerable discussions with groups of executives about their best experience. For a classic review of the tactics available for dealing with resistance, see John P. Kotter and Leonard A. Schlesinger (1979), 'Choosing Strategies for Change', *Harvard Business Review*. March-April 106–14.

Chapter 3

Most of the description of the quality improvement programme at Federal Express, and all the quotes, are from Christopher Lovelock (1990), 'Federal Express: Quality Improvement Program', *IMD Case* No. GM456.

For more on the communication of change, see T.J. Larkin and Sandar Larkin (1994), *Communicating Change: Winning Employee Support for New Business Goals*. McGraw Hill, New York.

Chapter 4

Most of the Sun Life example is from Sandra Vandermerwe and Brenda Sutton (1995), 'Sun Life Assurance plc: Creating Sustainable Customer Advantage Through Services (A), (B), (C)', *IMD Case Studies* No. M480, M481, M482.

Chapter 5

For more on the Ljubljanska story, see David Oliver and Paul Strebel (1995), 'Ljubljanska Banka (A) and (B)', *IMD Case Nos.* GM605 and GM606.

For a complementary approach to dealing with resistors, see R.M. Bramson (1981), *Coping with Difficult People*.

Chapter 6

In addition to the account provided by one of the key actors, most of the Spaarbeleg story and all the quotes are taken from J.M.B. Kassarjian (1992), 'Shaping Spaarbeleg: Real and Unreal', *IMD Case Study*, GM 537.

For more on what is needed for effective leadership, see F. J. House (1971), 'A Path-Goal Theory of Leadership Effectiveness', *Administrative Science Quarterly*. Sept, 321–38; John P. Kotter (1990), *A Force for Change: How Leadership Differs from Management*. The Free Press; S. Green and T. Mitchell (1979), 'Attributional Processes of Leaders in Leader–Member Interactions', *Organizational Behavior and Human Performance*. June, 429–58; R. Quinn, S. Faerman, M. Thompson and M. McGrath (1990), *Becoming A Master Manager*. New York: John Wiley & Son.

PART II

Chapter 7

The four classic change processes have been distilled out of Paul Strebel (1994), 'Choosing the right change path', *California Management Review*, 36, No. 2, 29–51 and Paul Strebel and Liisa Valikangas (1994), *International Review of Strategic Management*, Vol. 5, as well as Paul Strebel (1992), *Breakpoints: How Managers Exploit Radical Business Change*. Harvard Business School Press.

For complementary perspectives, see especially, J.N. Fry and P.K. Killing (1989), *Strategic Analysis and Action*, 2nd. edn. New Jersey, Prentice Hall, Chap 12; Yvan Allaire and Mikaela Firsirotu (1985), 'How to Implement Radical Strategies in Large Organizations', *Sloan Management Review*, Spring, 19–34; D. R. Denison (1990), *Corporate Culture and Organizational Effectiveness*. New York, John Wiley & Sons.

For more on the different types of change process, see Linda S. Ackerman (1986), *OD Practitioner*. Vol. 18, No. 4, December. Also, see T. Jick (1993), *Managing Change: Cases and Concepts* (Homewood, IL, Irwin 2; T. G. Cummings and C.G. Worley (1993), *Organization Development and Change*. 5th edn. Minneapolis/St. Paul, West; N.M.Tichy and M. A. DeVanna (1986), *The Transformational Leader*. New York, John Wiley & Sons; James Quinn (1980), 'Managing Strategic Change', *Sloan Management Review*, Summer.

Chapter 8

The Philips story is a synthesis from management development experience with the company, plus Philips Electronics N.V., *Annual Reports 1989–1994*, and 'Operation Centurion: Movement for Change', *de Nederlands* October 30, 1990; Hans Crooijmans (1995), 'Timmers tijd is voorbij', *Elsevier*, 18 February 60–5.

The leadership styles in this and the next three chapters are modelled on the leadership types described by P. Hersey and K. Blanchard (1988), *Management of Organizational Behavior*. 5th edn. New Jersey, Prentice-Hall; and their work, P. Hersey and K. Blanchard (1988), 'So You Want to Know Your Leadership Style?' *Training and Development Journal*, Feb. 22–32; and L. J. Bourgeois and David Brodwin (1983), 'Putting Your Strategy into Action', in *Strategic Management Journal*. March/May.

Chapter 9

The Medoil story is a disguised account of the change process at an oil and gas subsidiary of a major multinational, based on the experience of the change leader.

For the classic on process re-engineering, see M. Hammer and J. Champy (1993), *Reengineering the Corporation, A Manifesto for Business Revolution*. New York, Harper Business.

Chapter 10

The Ford of Europe story is based on discussions with managers during the changes, some of the earlier of which are reflected in Paul Strebel (1984), 'Ford of Europe', *IMD Case Study*, No. GM 321/322 and Paul Strebel (1985), 'How Ford of Europe reduced its Financial Staff Headcount', *International Management*, October, 120–8.

In a seminar-based approach to participative change, Jean-Phillippe Deschamps has emphasized the importance of a shared awareness of the need for change, shared understanding of what has to be done, and a shared commitment to action.

Chapter 11

The story of the Performance Chemicals Division is based on discussions with managers during the change, some of which are included in the disguised case study by Paul Strebel (1987), 'Betachem Energy Chemicals Division A&B', *IMD Case Study*, No. OIE 062/063.

For more on bottom-up change, see Michael Beer, Russell A. Eisenstat and Bert Grector (1990), 'Why Change Programs Don't Produce Change', *Harvard Business Review*. Nov/Dec 158–66.

Chapter 12

The material in this chapter was first published in Paul Strebel (1997), 'The Politics of Change', *IMD Perspectives for Managers*. Issue No.2, February. The Continental Auto story is a disguised case of change at a major car manufacturer, based on consulting experience.

For complementary approaches to the politics of change, see John P. Kotter (1978), 'Power, Success and Organizational Effectiveness', *Organizational Dynamics*, Winter; K. Kumar and M. Thibodeaux (1990), 'Organizational Politics and Planned Organizational Change', *Group and Organizational Studies*. Vol. 15, No. 4, 357–65; D.A. Nadler and M. L. Tushman (1979), 'A Congruence Model for Diagnosing Organizational Behavior', in D. Kolf, I. Rubin, and J. McIntyre, *Organizational Psychology: A Book of Readings*, 3rd. edn. New Jersey, Prentice Hall; Noel Tichy (1982), *Strategic Change Management*. New York, Wiley.

PART III

Chapter 13

In addition to discussions with managers who lived through the change, the story of AT&T Global Business Systems relies on Nick Obolensky (1994), 'AT&T Global Business Communication Systems', *Practical Business Re-Engineering: Tools and Techniques for Achieving Effective Change*. London, Kogan Page, Chap. 1.

The Siemens Nixdorf case is based on Mark Maletz (1997), 'Siemens Nixdorf's new dynamism', *Mastering Enterprise*. London, Financial Times Pitman 334–9, plus discussions with the management development consultants involved.

The IBM story reflects the experience of the change leader.

Chapter 14

The British Nuclear Fuels story is a synthesis of accounts from managers at the company and Paul Rowson (1995/96), 'Integrating the Improvement Process into the Mainstream of the Business', *Focus on Change Management*. Dec. 1995/Jan. 1996, 13–17.

The GE story is a synthesis from numerous sources, including managers at GE, plus the following: R. Slater (1983), *The New GE – How Jack Welch revived an American Institution*, Homewood, Illinois, Richard D. Irwin; Noel Tichy, S. Sherman (1993), *Control your own Destiny or Someone Else Will*. New York, Doubleday; Terence P. Pare (1994), 'GE Monkeys with its Money Machine', *Fortune*, 21 February, 43; and Valikangas Liisa (1994), 'Leading a Strategic Transformation at the Top', *Acta Universitatis Tamperensis*. Ser. A, Vol. 433.

The description of 3M's social compact for bottom-up initiatives is based mainly on its web site: http://www.mmm.com, with quotes from Roger Trapp (1997), '3M: back to the future', *MBA*, Vol. 1, No. 1, December, 40–7.

For more on the values and informal rules in an organization, see W. G. Ouchi and A.M. Jaeger (1978), 'Type Z Organizations: Stability in the Midst of Mobility', *Academy of Management Review*. Vol. 3, 308; R. E. Quinn (1988), *Beyond Rational Management*. San Francisco, Jossey-

Bass; E. Hall (1976), *Beyond Culture*. Garden City, N.Y., Anchor Press; The role of informal organizational rules in change management has been developed at some length by P. Scott-Morgan (1994), *The Unwritten Rules of the Game*. New York, McGraw Hill.

Chapter 15

The Granite Rock example is taken from John Case (1992), 'The Change Masters: Company Profile', *Inc*. March, 59–70. In addition to a first hand account, the Oticon story and all the quotes are from R. Morgan Gould, Michael Stanford, and Kate Blackmon (1994), 'Revolution at Oticon A/S: The Spaghetti Organization (Condensed)', *IMD Case Study* No. OB235; the CBIC example comes from Thomas A. Stewart (1994), 'Your Company's Most Valuable Asset: Intellectual Capital', *Fortune*, 3 October; and the Skandia example mainly from David Oliver, Donald A. Marchand, and Johan Roos (1995), 'Skandia Assurance Financial Services (A): Measuring Intellectual Capital, and (B): Managing Intellectual Capital', *IMD Case Studies* Nos. GM624 and GM625.

For the classic on learning organizations, see Peter Senge (1990), *The Fifth Discipline*. New York, Doubleday Currency and Peter Senge (1990), 'The Leader's New Work: Building Learning Organizations', *Sloan Management Review*. Fall; also Daniel H. Kim (1993), 'The Link between Individual and Organizational Learning', *Sloan Management Review*. Fall, 37–50.

Chapter 16

The Hewlett Packard story is complied from the following sources: discussions with HP managers, plus Richard King and Howard H. Stevenson (1983), 'Hewlett Packard: Challenging the Entrepreneurial Culture', *Harvard Business School Case Study* No. 9-384-035; Richard King and Howard H. Stevenson (1995), 'Hewlett Packard: Big, Boring and Booming', *The Economist*, 6 May, 69–70; Burrows Peter (1995), 'The Printer King Invades Home PCs: Can Latecomer Hewlett Packard leapfrog over the field?', *Business Week*. 21 August, 50–1; and Louise Kehoe (1994), 'Change while you are ahead: Hewlett Packard is in good shape but its chief executive is fighting complacency', *Financial Times*. 18 March, 12.

For more on the new adaptable, networked organization, see Jay Galbraith (1996), 'The Reconfigurable Organization', *Working Paper*; W. Halal (1994), 'From Hierarchy To Enterprise: Internal Markets Are the New Foundation of Management', *Academy of Management Executive*. Vol. 8 No. 4; Richard T. Pascale (1990), *Managing on the Edge*, New York, Touchstone: Simon & Schuster; Larry Greiner (1971), 'Evolution and Revolution as Organizations Grow', *Harvard Business Review*. July/August.

Additional references to outpacing the competition by altering the emphasis on innovation and efficiency include Xavier Gilbert and Paul Strebel (1987), 'Strategies to Outpace the Competition', *Journal of Business Strategy*. Summer, 28–37; Paul Strebel (1992), *Breakpoints*. Harvard Business School Press Part III; Paul Strebel and Christopher Parker (1988), 'Rebalancing the Organization: Key to Outpacing the Competition', *IMD Perspectives for Managers*. No. 3.

Chapter 17

For more on the way the new networked economy is affecting what people are looking for, see Douglas C. Henton, John Melville, and Kimberly Walesh (1997), *Grass Roots Leaders for a New Economy*. Jossey-Bass, and on the benefit of combining value creation with a larger purpose, see James C. Collins and Jerry I. Porras (1997), *Built to Last: Successful Habits of Visionary Companies*. Harper Business.

The basic features of an outpacing organization are summarized in Paul Strebel (1994), 'Proactive Breakpoints: Taking Charge of Your Industry', *IMD Perspectives for Managers*. No. 5, November, and Paul Strebel (1997), 'Creating Industry Breakpoints,' *Mastering Management*. Financial Times Pitman Publishing Module 17, 548–52.

Appendix 1

The value preferences used here come from those developed by Geert Hofstede (1983), 'The Cultural Relativity of Organizational Practices and Theories', *Journal of International Business Studies*. Fall, 75–89 and Charles Hampden-Turner and Alfons Trompenaars (1993), *The Seven Cultures of Capitalism*.

INDEX